Honor-Based Violence

Policing and Prevention

Honor-Based Violence

Violence

Policing and Prevention

Karl Anton Roberts
Gerry Campbell
Glen Lloyd

CRC Press
Taylor & Francis Group
Boca Raton London New York

CRC Press is an imprint of the
Taylor & Francis Group, an **informa** business

CRC Press
Taylor & Francis Group
6000 Broken Sound Parkway NW, Suite 300
Boca Raton, FL 33487-2742

First issued in paperback 2019

ISBN-13: 978-1-4665-5665-2 (hbk)
ISBN-13: 978-0-367-86743-0 (pbk)

Library of Congress Cataloging-in-Publication Data

Roberts, Karl Anton.
   Honor-based violence : policing and prevention / Karl Anton Roberts, Gerry Campbell, Glen Lloyd.
      pages cm. -- (Advances in police theory and practice ; 19)
   Includes bibliographical references and index.
   ISBN 978-1-4665-5665-2 (hardback)
   1. Women--Crimes against--Great Britain--Prevention. 2. Women--Crimes against--Great Britain. 3. Women's rights--Great Britain. I. Campbell, Gerry, 1967- II. Lloyd, Glen. III. Title.

HV6250.4.W65R632 2013
363.32--dc23
                                                2013018865

Visit the Taylor & Francis Web site at
http://www.taylorandfrancis.com

and the CRC Press Web site at
http://www.crcpress.com

This book is dedicated to my wife, Victoria, and to my parents, Jean and Brian, with all my love. KR

This book is dedicated to my wife, Gaye, and my children, Sarah, Ben, and Katie, with all my love. GL

Contents

4   Effective Investigation of Honor-Based Violence 2: Secondary Investigation   59

Series Editor's Preface

While the literature on police and allied subjects is growing exponentially its impact upon day-to-day policing remains small. The two worlds of research and practice of policing remain disconnected even though cooperation between the two is growing. A major reason is that the two groups speak in different languages. The research work is published in hard-to-access journals and presented in a manner that is difficult to comprehend for a layperson. On the other hand the police practitioners tend not to mix with researchers and remain secretive about their work. Consequently, there is little dialogue between the two and almost no attempt to learn from one another. Dialog across the globe, among researchers and practitioners situated in different continents, are of course even more limited.

I attempted to address this problem by starting the IPES, www.ipes.info, where a common platform has brought the two together. IPES is now in its 17th year. The annual meetings which constitute most major annual event of the organization have been hosted in all parts of the world. Several publications have come out of these deliberations and a new collaborative community of scholars and police officers has been created whose membership runs into several hundreds.

Another attempt was to begin a new journal, aptly called *Police Practice and Research: An International Journal*, *PPR*, that has opened the gate to practitioners to share their work and experiences. The journal has attempted to focus upon issues that help bring the two on a single platform.

Clearly, these attempts, despite their success, remain limited. Conferences and journal publications do help create a body of knowledge and an association of police activists but cannot address substantial issues in depth. The limitations of time and space preclude larger discussions and more authoritative expositions that can provide stronger and broader linkages between the two worlds.

It is this realization of the increasing dialogue between police research and practice that has encouraged many of us—my close colleagues and I connected closely with IPES and *PPR* across the world—to conceive and implement a new attempt in this direction. I have embarked on a book series, Advances in Police Theory and Practice, that seeks to attract writers from all parts of the world. Further, the attempt is to find practitioner contributors. The objective is to make the series a serious contribution to our knowledge of the police as well as to improve police practices. The focus is not only on work that describes the best and successful police practices but also one that challenges current paradigms and breaks new ground to prepare police for the twenty-first century. The series seeks comparative analysis that highlights achievements in distant parts of the world as well as one that encourages an in-depth examination of specific problems confronting a particular police force.

The current book is the product of a unique collaboration between an academic psychologist and two serving police officers who have, over a number of years, brought together their particular areas of expertise in order to develop effective methods of policing HBV. *Honor-Based Violence: Policing and Prevention* (Karl Anton Roberts, Gerry Campbell, and Glen Lloyd), will fulfill a long-felt need as a source of understanding, guidance and appropriate response to law enforcement officers as well as others who are working in the sphere of honor-based violence (HBV). Readers will find a wealth of information for understanding how to recognize HBV as well as how to provide support and sustenance to the victims, families and communities affected by it. True, HBV has been continuing since the hoary days of yore but only in recent times it has become a matter of concern to law enforcement and related agencies in the Western countries because of the cross-cultural movement of people across the globe. This is a timely contribution befitting the Advances in Police Theory and Practice Series.

It is hoped that through this series it will be possible to accelerate the process of building knowledge about policing and help bridge the gap between the two worlds: the world of police research and police practice. This is an invitation to police scholars and practitioners across the world to come and join in this venture.

Dilip K. Das, PhD
Founding President, International Police Executive Symposium
http://www.ipes.info

Series Editor, Advances in Police Theory and Practice
(CRC Press/Taylor & Francis Group)

Series Editor, Interviews with Global Leaders in Police, Courts, and Prisons
(CRC Press/Taylor & Francis Group)

Series Editor, PPR Special Issues as Books
(Routledge/Taylor & Francis Group)

Founding Editor-in-Chief, Police Practice and Research:
An International Journal (Routledge/Taylor & Francis Group)
http://www.tandfonline.com/GPPR

Prologue

This book is the product of a unique collaboration between an academic psychologist (Roberts) and two serving police officers (Lloyd and Campbell). The authors Lloyd and Campbell have together worked at the forefront of honor-based violence (HBV) policing policy development and implementation in a large United Kingdom police force and have had considerable experience investigating and managing cases of HBV. Roberts is a forensic psychologist and has spent many years advising law enforcement and government on behavioural issues relevant to police investigations and the development of policing policy. The collaboration between the authors grew out of their mutual interest in improving policing practice by bringing to bear knowledge and expertise from a range of disciplines on contemporary policing challenges. Over the years these authors have met regularly and discussion has frequently centered upon how the behavioural sciences can complement policing expertise in the investigation and management of crimes such as HBV. Ultimately the genesis of this book was a decision by the authors that it was time to capture some of the fruits of their collaboration and present them to a wider audience. Policing HBV is an attempt to respond to the challenges faced by law enforcement in dealing with this type of offending especially in an international context where there is little guidance on best practice. Indeed, while there are a few books that explore the sociocultural roots of HBV, there are no books that have a specific focus upon policing honor-based violence.

This book then, is an attempt to present the reader with the fruits of a long-standing collaboration—an account of best practice in the investigation and management of HBV.

About the Authors

Karl Roberts is a forensic psychologist who is currently director of research at the Centre for Policing, Intelligence, and Counter Terrorism at Macquarie University in Sydney, Australia. He also has a joint appointment as associate professor of criminal justice at the University of Massachusetts, Lowell. His specific areas of expertise are within the broad field of interpersonal violence and law enforcement investigation focusing on psychological and behavioral assessment of offenders, investigative interviewing, and threat assessment and management. He has particular interests in the psychology of honor and honor-based violence, and threat identification and management of violent crimes, such as stalking and honor-based crimes. He also has expertise in investigative interviewing by law enforcement and other agencies and has published a number of papers on this. Roberts works closely with law enforcement and other agencies throughout Australia, the United Kingdom, Europe, and the United States providing training and advice to investigations in the form of threat assessments and investigative strategies. To date, he has provided advice to over 450 major police investigations.

Gerry Campbell is detective chief superintendent with 26 years of service in London's Metropolitan Police Service (MPS). He is currently leading a borough as the borough commander in central Inner London. He also is currently the United Kingdom's Association of Chief Officer's deputy lead for honor-based violence, forced marriage, and female genital mutilation. He co-authored ACPO's first honor-based strategy. Campbell has led Scotland Yard's policy development relating to public protection including domestic violence (including DV (domestic violence) homicide review), honor-based violence, hate crime, and the management of registered sexual offenders and dangerous offenders while leading high-risk operations. He has chaired and led a number of strategic groups relating to these crime genres and has been an important part of key national strategy groups. Campbell has worked with the U.K. government and law enforcement, and NGO colleagues from around the world including the United States, Sweden, Denmark, Germany, Iraqi Kurdistan, Pakistan, and Australia.

Glen Lloyd is a detective chief inspector in London's Metropolitan Police Service (MPS). He is currently working as a senior investigating officer in the Homicide and Serious Crime Command where his responsibilities include murder and other serious crime investigations. In his 21 years of service, Lloyd has served in some of London's most challenging boroughs, investigating a wide variety of crimes as well as managing many criminal investigation departments from major crime, burglary, and robbery as well as within the field of public protection. It was within the area of public protection when Lloyd became aware of and interested in honor-based violence (HBV) crimes. This interest was further enhanced when he worked with co-author Gerry Campbell in the MPS' Violent Crime Directorate where they had the lead for service delivery of HBV across the MPS. This involved working with Her Majesty's (HM) government, ACPO (Association of Chief Police Officers), strategic partners, and nongovernmental organizations (NGOs) in developing and enhancing the MPS' response to HBV. This included providing both tactical and strategic advice on many and some of the most high profile HBV investigations in London and the United Kingdom.

Acknowledgments

In writing a book such as this, there are many people to whom we would like to pay tribute and to offer sincere thanks for their help.

First, we would like to offer thanks to the editorial team at Taylor & Francis Group, Dr. Dilip Das, Advances in Police Theory and Practice series editor; Carolyn Spence, senior acquisitions editor; Jennifer Ahringer, project coordinator, and two anonymous manuscript reviewers for all their work and the useful comments and suggestions that have, we think, greatly improved this book. We also would like to thank all of our colleagues who have, over the years, worked with us and helped us in ways both large and small to develop our thoughts and ideas about honor and violence committed in its name. Karl Roberts would particularly like to thank Dr. Victoria Herrington for contributing her time and expertise to discuss some of the concepts contained herein and for providing, as always, some insightful comments and good ideas.

We would especially like to take this opportunity to acknowledge all of the police officers and police staff working within Community Safety Units (CSUs) who often go above and beyond the call of duty to keep victims safe and hold perpetrators to account for their actions. We also would like to acknowledge the nongovernmental organizations (NGOs) that work within this field. These agencies work in a context of little funding and sometimes much community resistance to offer support to the victims of HBV, sharing their knowledge with the police and others so that vulnerable victims may be better protected.

Finally, we would like to pay tribute to all of the victims of so-called honor-based violence. It is through their suffering that the police and others have learned many important lessons and improved their ability to respond to these crimes.

In thanking others for their contributions to the development of this book, it goes without saying that any errors or omissions are those of the authors.

Introduction

Surjit Athwal, a 27-year-old Sikh woman, worked as a customs officer at Heathrow Airport in London. She disappeared after going to a family wedding in India in December 1998. Her mother-in-law, Bachan Athwal, ordered Surjit's death at a family meeting after discovering that she had been having an affair and wanted a divorce from her son.

Samaira Nazir, a 25-year-old British Pakistani, recruitment consultant, died after she tried to escape her family home following a row over her plans to marry an Afghan asylum seeker whom the family deemed as being "unsuitable." Her brother, Azhar Nazir, 30, dragged her back into the house where he and his distant cousin, Imran Mohammed, 17, worked together to hold her down and stab her to death. Her throat was cut and she was stabbed 18 times in the attack that used four knives. Samaira's mother also helped to hold her down during the attack. This attack was performed in front of other family members, including two of Samaira's nieces.

A 14-year-old Greenfield, California resident, Maria, was sold by her father into marriage with an 18-year-old man in exchange for 100 cases of beer and a few cases of meat. When her new spouse failed to deliver the promised goods, Maria's father called police to retrieve his daughter and bring her home. But, not before Maria's husband earned statutory rape charges by consummating the marriage.

"Anita" describes her experiences of female genital mutilation. "When I was 'circumcised.' I was 5 or 6. The equipment they use is handmade: a sharp curved knife, which is not sterilized. And I was given no anesthetic. They left a little hole for urination. There were no stitches, but they treated the wound with herbs, salt, and water. It bled a lot and I was in great pain. I was horribly frightened and crying" (United Kingdom Foreign and Commonwealth Office, 2011).

All of these cases involve terrible acts of violence toward or gross neglect of a victim by family members. They are all the more shocking because they are acts perpetrated or encouraged by family members against their own for what appears to be no good reason. What could they possibly gain from these acts?

What the cases all have in common is that they were motivated by concerns about individual and family honor; they are examples of so-called honor-based violence, carried out to preserve or regain family honor that was threatened. Surjit Athwal was murdered because she "dishonored" and shamed her family by having an affair and wanting a divorce. Samaira Nazir died because she "dishonored" and shamed her family by having a relationship with an "unsuitable" individual. Maria's father failed to protect her from rape by selling her because it was his right as a father to do so, and he would have been "dishonored" had she failed to behave in accordance with his wishes. The young child experienced painful, unnecessary, and potentially life-threatening surgery in a family's desire to maintain their honor and preserve tradition.

Though honor-based violence (HBV) has existed for thousands of years, it is only very recently, through cases such as these, that it has become of concern to law enforcement and other agencies in Western countries. Indeed, many law enforcement officers and workers in the statutory and voluntary sectors are still unsure what HBV is, how to investigate it, and how to support victims.

This book, therefore, has been written to assist all of those people working in the law enforcement, statutory, or voluntary sector to understand honor-based violence. It sets out to explain what HBV is, how it can be recognized, and how we can support the victims, families, and communities that experience it.

Many people will consider the use of the term *honor-based violence* as abhorrent when viewed in the context of a victim's suffering and the seriousness of the crimes committed in the name of honor. The authors understand and are sympathetic to this sentiment. However, while we want to make it clear our view is that there is indeed no "honor" in HBV, it is important in a book such as this to provide a label that clearly identifies the issue at hand and differentiates it from other forms of violence. The term *honor-based violence*, therefore, is used because it has been used in previous literature as a label for this form of violence and to illustrate that this violence is committed by perpetrators in the mistaken view that it will somehow preserve or bring them "honor."

It is hoped the following chapters will give the reader an understanding of what HBV is in all of its many manifestations. We provide an overview of what is known about the psychological and cultural factors relevant to understanding HBV and explore the investigation and management of honor-based violence; this from the primary investigating officer through to secondary investigating officers and the strategic management of HBV cases. We also aim to give the reader an insight into risk assessment and risk management of HBV and how working in partnership can reduce risk, support investigations, and help protect victims.

Honor-Based Violence: Policing and Prevention draws upon the experience of the authors who have had practical, tactical, and strategic exposure to HBV over many years. Although we make use of extant academic and other literatures, many of the suggestions and recommendations we make are necessarily made on the basis of this experience and are made because they have been successful strategies in dealing with HBV. Throughout the book, we acknowledge the important need to be sensitive toward differences in race, culture, and religion. However, we do stress that this should not be at the expense of protecting vulnerable individuals, protecting children, or holding perpetrators to account for breaking the law.

Ultimately, if this book helps to reduce the suffering caused by HBV or even saves just one life, then we will have achieved everything we hoped for in writing it.

Karl Roberts
Gerry Campbell
Glen Lloyd

What Is Honor-Based Violence? 1

In this chapter, we will define honor-based violence (HBV) and describe the types of offending that fall within this definition. The chapter also will present details about the prevalence of different forms of HBV, the characteristics of victims and perpetrators, and the impact of HBV. We begin by providing a definition of honor-based violence.

Defining Honor-Based Violence

Important to any discussion of honor-based violence (HBV) is first an understanding of what is meant by *honor*. Honor is most often defined as a virtue or character trait that is associated with integrity, good moral character, and altruism with individuals being described in terms of having *honor* or being considered *honorable* (Vandello & Cohen, 2003). Having honor is a positive state and confers with it many advantages, in particular trust and respect from others. There is also a second, albeit less common, definition of honor that sees it as linked to status and reputation (Pitt-Rivers, 1966) and is based on a person's ability, strength, and power to enforce his or her will on and to command respect from others (Nisbett & Cohen, 1996). So, rather than being simply a character trait, honor within this definition is something that has to be fought for and jealously guarded. While this second conception of honor is less common, there is considerable evidence that it is held with some conviction by a substantial number of individuals (see Evolution of Honor Cultures in Chapter 2). It is this focus upon obtaining and defending honor that appears to be a core motivation for HBV.

Given this definition of honor, how then do we define HBV? There is considerable debate about the definition of HBV and little agreement has so far been reached within the literature. This lack of agreement is problematic, especially for practitioners trying to make sense of the literature. For example, where authors have used different definitions of HBV, it is difficult to compare findings, and this means that generalizations are problematic. The definitions of HBV that do exist range from narrow and highly specific (encompassing relatively few crime types and defining specific victims and perpetrators) to broader definitions encompassing a wider range of crime types, victims, and perpetrators. Narrow definitions have the advantage that they directly specify the context of HBV and do not become bogged down with overgeneralizing the behavior; however, they run the risk that they may miss features of HBV that are interesting and relevant. For example, many definitions of HBV define it exclusively as a form of violence against women (Hossain & Welchman, 2005), with writers, such as Meetoo and Mirza (2007), among others, defining HBV exclusively as a form of domestic violence by men against women. This narrow definition directs attention to just one type of perpetrator and victim. However, as we shall see, there are male victims of HBV and female perpetrators; therefore these forms of HBV are explicitly neglected by this definition. Also, HBV appears to involve a range of other behavior that is not traditionally classified as domestic violence such as forced marriage and female genital mutilation. In contrast, broader definitions of HBV encompass much more behavior and a wider range of contexts, although they have the risk of overreporting HBV. For example, the definition of HBV provided by the U.K. Association of Chief Police Officers (ACPO) is gender neutral and is not specific as to what criminality is included, which allows for a wider range of behavior to be classified as HBV. ACPO defines HBV as:

> ... a crime or incident, which has or may have been committed to protect or defend the honor of the family and/or community (ACPO, 2010a).

For the purposes of this book, we wish to provide a definition of HBV that is clear and succinct and that is as unrestrictive as possible so that we can consider the full range of perpetrators, victims, and crime types who practitioners are likely to encounter. As such, the definition of HBV that we will use in the book is the ACPO definition detailed above. It is important to note that we are not making an uncritical acceptance of this definition; there are many caveats to it. For example, the question arises of how do we *know* or indeed can we ever *know* unequivocally when a crime has been committed to defend or protect family honor, since this is a judgment concerning motivation for offending, which is notoriously difficult to assess? However, as we will see in this book, crimes of honor do have some identifiable characteristics.

In addition, within our definition of HBV, any violent crime that is motivated by concerns with honor, in principle, could be classed as HBV, as long as the aim is to protect family or community honor. This could include gang-related violence (if the gang is considered a community). However, there is, in practice, a narrower range of crime types that are associated with the term *honor-based violence* and these are crimes committed mostly within a family/domestic violence context. Therefore, we will explicitly exclude consideration of gang and similar types of violence in our discussion. Hossain and Welchman (2005) identify several types of HBV including *murder (honor killings), assault, confinement or imprisonment, and interference with choice in marriage.* In addition, other activities also have been included, such as *female genital mutilation, female infanticide,* some forms of *child abuse,* and *selective female abortion.*

To enhance the reader's knowledge and understanding of the range of offending associated with HBV, we now move on to consider the characteristics of these crimes. For many of the crime types described, there is little systematic research and so much of this discussion is based on the experience of the authors as practitioners working in the field of HBV.

Crime Types Associated With HBV

In this section, we will describe the characteristics of a number of crime types commonly associated with HBV. Here, we will group crime types around a number of themes, which are broadly associated with the perpetrators, targets, and the stage of a victim's life when the violence is most likely.

HBV Directed Toward Children

In some families, preference for male children exists. In these families, males are perceived to be of higher value and status than females. This is often because males are seen as being more likely, when older, to bring higher wages to the family home to support the parents and other family members. Males also may be seen as being vital to carrying on a family's lineage. Females, on the other hand, may be seen as a financial and social liability to the family. This may be because cultural traditions dictate the provision of a financial dowry when a daughter marries, or females may be less able to support the family financially due to childbirth later in their lives. As a result of the value attached to male children, a number of criminal acts may be directed toward female children in the name of *honor.* The violence in these cases is most likely to be perpetrated by parents and includes the following types:

Sex-Selective Abortion

Due to the perceived importance of male offspring for some families, family members may establish the sex of an unborn child. In the event the unborn child is female, they may attempt to arrange an abortion. Sex-selective abortion is illegal in most Western countries, though some parents may get around the legislation by shielding the true reasons for an abortion or by travelling abroad where they may find doctors sympathetic to the family's beliefs and/ or who may work for financial reward to terminate the pregnancy. Related to selective abortion in the attempt to dispose of a female baby is the practice of female infanticide—the killing of female children under the age of 1 year—or abandonment of female children.

Child Abuse and Neglect

Where male children are regarded as most important, female children may face abuse and neglect by virtue of their sex and may be explicitly denied the same opportunities as males. Females may be denied education or may be prevented from finishing statutory education. Females also may be restricted in other activities from an early age where they may be "policed" by male members of the family; their movements and behavior restricted, and any transgression met with violent punishment, confinement, or being denied food.

Female Genital Mutilation (FGM)

FGM (also referred to as *female genital cutting, female circumcision,* or *initiation*) is a surgical procedure often carried out by older female members of a family or members of the broader community. The procedure includes the total or partial removal of the external female genitalia.

The World Health Organization (2012) has classified FGM into four types:

1. Type 1—Clitoridectomy: Partial or total removal of the clitoris[*] and, in rare cases, only the prepus.[†]
2. Type 2—Excision: Partial or total removal of the clitoris and the labia minor, with or without excision of the labia majora.[‡]
3. Type 3—Infibulation: Narrowing of the vaginal opening through the creation of a covering seal. The seal is formed by cutting and repositioning the inner, or outer labia, with or without the removal of the clitoris.
4. Type 4—Other: All other harmful procedures to the female genitalia for nonmedical purposes, e.g., pricking, piercing, incising, scraping, and cauterizing the genital area.

The age at which FGM is carried out varies greatly ranging from a newborn girl, during childhood or adolescence, just before marriage, or during the first pregnancy. However, it would appear the majority of FGM takes place when girls are between 5 and 8 years of age.

It is estimated that, worldwide, around 140 million women and girls have undergone FGM, 92 million of them in Africa. FGM is particularly prevalent in central African communities where there is a 40% prevalence rate. These nations include Somalia, Guinea, Djibouti, Sierra Leone, Egypt, Sudan, Eritrea, Mali, The Gambia, Ethiopia, Burkina Faso, Mauritania, Liberia, Chad, and Guinea-Bissau. It also is seen in many other countries including some Arab States, India, Indonesia, Malaysia, and Pakistan (UNICEF, 2010). This practice is also found amongst communities within Western nations;

[*] Small, sensitive, and erectile part of the female genitals.
[†] The fold of skin surrounding the clitoris.
[‡] Labia: The lips that surround the vagina.

for example, it is estimated that in the United Kingdom, 66,000 women have undergone FGM, with 33,000 girls considered at risk every year (U.K. Foreign Office, 2011).

FGM has a significant impact upon the health and well-being of victims. The procedure is extremely painful and anesthetic often is not used. As the procedure is often carried out by untrained practitioners in unsterilized conditions, the practice can have serious health consequences at the time and later in life with victims suffering from infections of various types. Indeed, approximately 10% of girls die from the immediate consequences of undergoing FGM and 25% face an early death as a result of the long-term consequences (U.K. Foreign Office, 2011).

A girl who has been subjected to FGM may have problems sitting, standing, or walking; she may suffer bladder problems and may have problems urinating, therefore, spending more time in the bathroom; menstrual problems are also common. Girls who have suffered FGM may have a history of repeated or prolonged absences from school, and may be reluctant to be medically examined. Rarely, victims may confide in a professional or may ask for help without being specific due to fear or embarrassment.

FGM is a complex issue with a wide variety of explanations and motives for its practice. It is often seen as a "natural" practice by advocates and in the "best" interest of the girls. Among individuals who engage in this practice, a number of common reasons are given in support of FGM, including:

- It brings status and respect to the girl.
- It preserves a girl's virginity/chastity.
- It cleanses and purifies the girl.
- It is part of being a woman.
- It is a rite of passage.
- It is customary.
- It gives a girl social acceptance, which is important especially for marriage.
- It gives the girl and her family a sense of belonging to the community.
- It fulfills a religious requirement (though no religious texts support FGM).
- It is cosmetically desirable.
- It is sometimes mistakenly believed to make childbirth safer for an infant.

In some cultures, FGM is an important *purity* characteristic of a would-be bride. In these cultures, in order for the girl to prove her purity to the husband, it is necessary for the husband and his family to see the girl "*closed*" (see Type 3 FGM above). Later it can be the responsibility of mothers to take the girl to be *"opened"* sufficiently to be able to have sexual intercourse with her spouse.

FGM, therefore, seems to be used as a means of protecting the female and her honor and of avoiding bringing shame on the family. It should be noted here that, as with other forms of HBV, while many readers may view these reasons for FGM as misguided, if not abhorrent, it is important to consider that they represent powerful beliefs and attitudes for some individuals that can serve to justify and encourage the behavior. Also, for some perpetrators, the cost of not engaging in these behaviors can be very high with a high risk of negative social sanctions from their community as well as economic losses, such as being unable to marry off a daughter. In policing this and other forms of HBV, it, therefore, is important that investigators and agencies recognize these beliefs and attitudes, their power, and the functions that they serve. Indeed another important effect of these attitudes and beliefs is that they limit the incentive of individuals to come forward and report the practice to authorities.

HBV Later in Life

As children grow into adults, further pressures and concerns may impinge upon a family. These concerns most typically focus upon daughters. Many of these relate to cultural practices and traditions associated with marriage and cultural expectations about appropriate behavior for women and girls. This may lead to HBV committed by a girl's family or by the family of her spouse. Here, we consider some of the types of HBV in this context.

Dowry

In some cultures, the provision of a sufficient dowry by a girl's family is crucial to finding a suitable husband. A dowry is the property that a wife brings to her husband and traditionally consisted of gifts, such as jewelry, to provide her with security following the marriage. Today, it is most common for a financial settlement to be paid by the bride's family to the groom's family. In some circumstances, the amount demanded can be excessive and demands for extra money can continue for months or years after the wedding. Irrespective of any financial difficulty, if a bride's family fails to meet these payments, the result can be severe abuse and harassment of their daughter. On occasion, new brides are killed because the dowry is insufficient or the bride may take her own life to spare her family further shame, hardship, or dishonor.

Bride Price

Related to the dowry is the bride price. This is the price that a groom's family will give to the bride's family. Though its intention is that of bringing two families together in a symbol of sincerity, good faith, and togetherness, it can lead to a groom and his family believing they have literally purchased the bride from her family and, therefore, they now *own* her. In some cases, this may predicate abuse, hostility, and violence leveled at the bride by both the groom and his family. This may ultimately lead to a bride committing suicide to prevent shame and loss of honor for her family or even homicide of the bride by her new family.

Forced Marriage

Forced marriage can be defined as:

> ... a marriage conducted without the valid consent of both parties where duress is a factor (HM Government, 2007).

It is important in any discussion of forced marriage to distinguish it from *arranged marriage*. In arranged marriages, while the families of both spouses take a leading role in arranging the marriage, the prospective spouses have a choice as to whether or not to accept the arrangements. In a forced marriage, one or both of the prospective spouses *do not* or *cannot* consent to the marriage. Duress can include verbal, psychological, emotional, physical, and financial pressure to force the marriage. It is particularly noteworthy that some individuals go ahead with a marriage because they are unaware they have a free choice to choose their spouse (Gill & Anitha, 2011). Forced marriage is relatively common even within Western nations; for example, in the United Kingdom, recent figures suggest a prevalence of reported forced marriage as 8,000 cases per year (DCSF, 2009).

When practitioners examine a marriage for validity, we advise that three "Cs" should be present: *Consent, Choice,* and *Compatibility.* That is, *consent* of both parties to the marriage, a *free choice* to accept the marriage or reject it, and *compatibility* between the parties especially in terms of age, background, and cultural experience. A forced marriage often will not have any of these three factors.

Though more females are subjected to a forced marriage, it is not uncommon for males to be victims of forced marriage.

Forced marriage has a significant impact upon its victims and can result in significant physical and emotional problems for victims. Forced marriage frequently includes physical and psychological abuse as well as social isolation at the hands of a spouse or his/her family. Physical and emotional abuse can occur where victims are beaten, criticized, and humiliated by their spouse's family. Physical and emotional abuse and social isolation can occur because victims frequently are forced to live as part of their spouse's family away from their own family and friends. They also may be actively prevented from contacting or socializing with others and from obtaining a job or taking educational opportunities. Social isolation also occurs when a victim is unable to speak the dominant language in the country in which he or she lives. This frequently means that he or she may be unaware of their legal rights and/or unable to report their experience to relevant authorities. Because of the social isolation inherent in forced marriage, individuals may rarely come to the attention of authorities through self-report and instead come to attention through other behavior consistent with distress, e.g., minor criminality, running away from home, inappropriate relationships, self harm, and alcohol and/or drug abuse.

It is also noteworthy that many victims of forced marriage often become victims of sexual abuse because their spouses wish to consummate their "marriage" and, due to subsequent sexual acts directed toward them.

Common justifications of parents for forcing their children into a marriage and for communities supporting this practice include:

- a desire to protect their children from negative cultural influences, e.g., being Westernized, drinking, drug taking;
- a desire to build stronger families;
- a desire to preserve cultural or religious traditions although it is important to note that there is no religious text that supports forced marriage; indeed every major faith states that consent is a prerequisite for all marriages;
- a response to pressure from extended families for children to be married;
- an attempt to fulfill agreements made when children were infants;
- to support entry into a country for a relative's children;
- to control unwanted sexuality; often forced marriage is targeted toward gay, lesbian, or transgender individuals in an attempt to "cure" them;
- to prevent unsuitable relationships;
- to strengthen family links;
- to achieve financial gain;
- to ensure assets including land, property, or financial wealth, stay within the family; and
- to ensure care for a child or adult (usually the victim of the forced marriage) with special needs when parents or existing careers are unable to fulfill that role.

Young girls who are forced into marriage are often withdrawn from education, restricting their social and educational development, and it is not unknown for girls as young as 5 to be forced into marriage. Another aspect of forced marriage is the practice of taking some girls overseas to be married. Many young girls will travel overseas with parents or other family members with no awareness that the plan is for them to marry. In some cases, girls will be left overseas with their intended or even the intended spouse's family for prolonged periods of time until they agree to marry.

Often for the victims of forced marriage, running away from the situation or suicide is their only option to reduce their suffering. However, victims are frequently in communities where they have few friends, they may not speak the language, and very few have the resources for life away the abusive families. This can compound feelings of isolation and may mean a return to the abusive environment. Similarly, when a victim of forced marriage leaves the home, or even contacts support agencies, this can be seen as bringing *dishonor* and shame onto the family. This, in turn, can result in social ostracism and harassment from other family members and members of the community. This can be a powerful incentive for the victim to stay in the marriage (Gill & Anitha, 2011).

For those who do succeed in escaping from a forced marriage, their families will often go to considerable lengths to find them and secure their return. Families, for example, will make use of community networks and even professional bounty hunters to track the individual down. Some families may even report the individual as a missing person for police to track him or her down for the family. In addition, the family may make false allegations of crimes to facilitate a police search for the victim. If found by families, the victims of forced marriage can become the victims of serious and prolonged physical and sexual attacks, which may culminate in them being killed.

Honor Killing

Honor killings are perhaps the most widely recognized form of HBV, thanks largely to significant media interest in this type of offending. Honor killings can be defined as:

> Murders in which victims, predominantly women, are killed for perceived immoral behavior, which is deemed to have breached the honor code of a family or community, causing shame " (Human Rights Watch, 2001).

This definition has been influential upon policing and was adopted by ACPO as their working definition in the United Kingdom.

In 2000, the United Nations estimated that there are 5,000 honor killings per year worldwide (United Nations, 2000). However, the general consensus is that this figure grossly underestimates the true figure. Indeed, some argue that this figure is a reasonable estimate of the prevalence of honor killings in Pakistan alone (Chesler, 2010). There are a number of reasons for this underestimation, but perhaps the most significant is that many of these murders are not classified as honor killings. Indeed, some jurisdictions, particularly in the West, are reluctant to classify murders of this type as honor-based (Chesler, 2010), and many activist groups reject the label *honor killing*, insisting instead that it (and all forms of HBV) are simply forms of broader domestic violence and should not be regarded as distinct (Chesler, 2010). It has been argued, however, that honor killings are a distinct type of violence with a distinct pattern of motivation and victimization and we, in writing this book, subscribe to this view (Chesler, 2010, and see Chapter 3).

Honor killings may be either an intended outcome, i.e., the offenders intend for the victim to die in an attack, or as an unintended consequence of some other honor-related abuse. There are a wide variety of events that may trigger an honor killing and these are broadly similar to those for other types of HBV. In the United Kingdom, the London Metropolitan Police have identified the following events:

- An unapproved relationship with a person who is unacceptable to the family
- The existence of a boyfriend/girlfriend
- An interfaith relationship
- Inappropriate dress or using makeup by the victim
- Rejecting a forced marriage
- Running away from home or an (abusive) marriage
- Seeking a divorce
- An extramarital affair
- Perceived sexual promiscuity on the victim's part
- Pregnancy outside of marriage
- Kissing or intimacy in a public space
- Truanting from school
- In response to a victim's objections to being removed from education
- A victim's rejection of religion or religious instruction
- The victim's sexual orientation be it gay, lesbian, transgender, or bisexual
- The victim was a victim of rape
- The victim reporting any abuse he or she experiences to the police or other authorities

Perpetrators of honor killings are most likely to be male family members, accounting for approximately 90% of all perpetrators (Chesler, 2010). Though it is generally males who are the perpetrators, females do take part in honor killings, most typically the mother of the victim. The role taken by females can be as active participants in the murder itself or in planning the murder and protecting other offenders. Evidence from some honor killings has shown as well the active involvement of a family matriarch in ordering others to carry out an honor killing.

In contrast to other forms of homicide, multiple perpetrators are also relatively common, accounting for approximately 20% of honor killings. Where there is more than one offender, this typically involves two or more family members, in particular, the victim's father and other male relatives, such as the victim's brother(s) and uncle(s). Less typically, although notable by its occurrence in a few case examples, the multiple perpetrators can be the victim's father and mother.

The majority of the victims of honor killings are females (approximately 90–95%; Chesler, 2010). However, males also may be victims of honor killings, often as a consequence of being involved in an "inappropriate" relationship with a female member of another family or as a consequence of their sexual orientation.

Typically, the victims of honor killings are young people with an average age of around 23 years. This is perhaps not surprising as this is an age group that is most likely to be challenging the authority of elders and is most active in dating and forming various social relationships, which is precisely the conditions most likely to be challenging to family "honor" as described above. These findings contrast with the general pattern of femicide in Western nonimmigrant populations where perpetrators are generally husbands acting alone.

Honor killings are often planned following a family council where male (or sometimes female) members of the family will decide whether the victim is guilty of what is alleged and the punishment he or she will receive. On occasion, younger males are used to commit the crime itself as it may be seen by some families as a "rite of passage" to adulthood, as a means of protecting older family members from being arrested, and in the belief that younger family members will receive a lesser punishment because of their age.

In approximately 1 to 2% of cases, contract killers may be employed by families to carry out the killing. The contract killers are often individuals from overseas who specialize in this type of violence and to preempt our discussion of risk factors for HBV, where individuals from overseas are observed to arrive in the family, this can be a sign that the family is planning an attack on a family member and that the attack may be imminent.

In some cases, if a decision has been made by the family to kill the victim, the victim may be taken abroad to countries that are more "sympathetic" to honor issues for the murder to be committed in order to enable perpetrators to have a better chance of evading justice. Again, from a risk perspective where a family is making plans to travel overseas, this may be a sign of a high risk of an attack on a victim.

Acid Attacks

Acid attacks generally involve throwing acid into the face and onto the body of the victim. This type of attack is typically directed toward females by males. Often the motives are derived from the attacker's sense of being dishonored by the victim and attacks can follow such things as the victim rejecting his attentions or proposals, family disputes centering on issues of marriage, or inadequate dowries. The intention appears to be to permanently disfigure the woman to prevent her attracting another man as a husband and/or to place an economic burden on the woman's family as they will then have to support her in the absence of a husband. Though rare in the western world, acid attacks appear to be most common in Asia. A related form of female disfigurement is damage to/removal of the victim's nose. There are a number of reports of this activity particularly from Afghanistan and parts of Pakistan; it is commonly used as a punishment for women by groups, such as the Taliban.

Blood Feuds

Blood feuds are feuds between different families that require the spilling of blood to restore family honor. These feuds can last for many years often creating a cycle of revenge that transcends the homeland of the perpetrators and moves into the areas where families have since settled.

A blood feud can be settled if the aggressor or his family agree to pay compensation to the aggrieved family; this may be in financial terms, land, property, or the exchange of a female member of the family. The nature of the compensation is often decided by an informal court made up of community members. Again, there is a strong emphasis upon the use of females as property that can be given away to assuage problems. Where a female family member is exchanged to end a blood feud, it is often the case that she is stigmatized by her new family and may suffer significant abuse as a result. Forced marriages, on occasion, can be an attempt to end a blood feud by marrying off a female family member to the aggrieved family.

It is worthy of note that women and even young girls can be sent or trafficked across international boundaries in reparation or penance of a blood feud. Often the victims will be intended as brides or domestic slaves (or both) for the destination family. An important note for investigators is that many of the females traveling can be children or girls in their early teens; travel documents may be altered to show individuals as older than they actually are.

Rape

In many cultures that emphasize honor, sexual victimization of a female through rape or indecent assault can be regarded as dishonoring her own family. In such families, no support will be afforded to her as a victim of sexual violence and she can become the victim of HBV including being killed. In some cases, the rape victim may be forced to marry her attacker to restore family honor. Some victims may commit suicide to rid themselves and their families of the shame and stigma of being a rape victim.

Girls that are forced into a marriage are often raped on their wedding night. This is often the first time they have met their groom and, regardless of their feelings or desire for him, the victim is expected to consummate the marriage on the wedding night.

Some cultures where honor is important also see rape itself as a form of punishment. The rape may be committed prior to an honor killing in order to shame the victim prior to her death, or a female may be raped for revenge and retribution in order to dishonor her whole family.

Impact of HBV

As we have discussed above, HBV involves considerable physical and emotional suffering on the part of victims and there are a number of outcomes that can result from it. In this section, we consider the impact of HBV upon victims and some of the self-injurious behaviors that victims may carry out that have been found to be particularly associated with HBV victimization. To date, no systematic research has been carried out upon the impact of HBV on victims and, thus, much of this section is derived from the experience of the authors in investigating cases of HBV.

Self-Harm

Many victims of HBV resort to self harm. Self harm is often hidden from others and may be a way of releasing unbearable feelings of anger, frustration, fear, and anxiety. Studies show that a higher percentage of South Asian women than other populations self harm, and there is a possibility that, as this is a cultural group in which there is a higher prevalence of HBV than other groups, this may be at least in part linked to the experience of HBV, isolation, and lack of support from families (Marshall & Yazdani, 1999).

Self-harm can occur in many ways; however, below are some of the methods of self-harm that have been seen by practitioners and which seem to be particularly common in victims of HBV:

- Depriving themselves of food
- Self cutting, especially on their arms, legs, or torso
- Burning themselves with fire or scolding water
- Hitting themselves
- Pulling out their own hair
- Swallowing poisons or noxious substances
- Forcing themselves to be physically sick

Practical experience with victims of HBV indicates that self-harm is relatively common for victims. However, this has not been systematically studied. It can be stated, though, that where suspected cases of HBV are being investigated, the presence of self-harm within the victim, while not in itself enough to confirm HBV, may in the absence of other obvious causes of self-harm be a possible indictor of HBV in a family. It also is important to note that where self-harm injuries are identified in a context of suspected HBV, authorities should be alert to the risk of suicide attempts by the victim.

Self-Immolation

Self-immolation is the act of setting fire to oneself. In some cases, self-immolation leads to death, although some individuals do survive often with severe, life-changing injuries. In the context of HBV, self-immolation typically represents a significant statement and protest against the victim's personal suffering. As it also causes shame for the victim's (and, if married, the spouse's) family, victims of HBV self-immolation also may be the only way for victims to "challenge" their abusers. Law enforcement agencies, when they come across self-immolation, need to note that it can be a sign that the victim was experiencing HBV, and so they would be advised to carry out a detailed investigation into the victim's background.

Suicide

The suicide of South Asian women is three times higher than that of women from other cultures and is similar to that of armed forces veterans coming home from theatres of war (McKenzie et al., 2008). While the reasons for suicide are likely to be varied, it is important not to overlook the possibility that suicide can be predicated upon experiences of HBV, especially when one considers that South Asian women are one of the groups at highest risk of HBV and the victims of HBV suffer significant emotional and physical abuse so suicide may be the only viable escape from this. With this in mind, it is important, however, to caution that investigators should not simply assume that, because someone from South Asia committed suicide, it indicates that she was an HBV victim. It is important, therefore, that when law enforcement officers attend a suicide where HBV is suspected, that the suicide is contextualized against the life history of the victim.

Where HBV is a factor, there appears to be at least two very good motives for the suicide. The first sees the suicide as an act of complete desperation in which the victim feels unable to escape from her abuse and death is the only viable way to end her suffering. Within HBV contexts, some families also will explicitly pressure the victim into committing suicide and may even provide the means to do this. It is important for investigators to note that some perpetrators of honor killings will attempt to stage a homicide so that it looks like a suicide or even self-immolation to attempt to disguise the offending.

As we will discuss in later chapters, investigators need to carry out a detailed investigation of all suicides where HBV is suspected to have been a factor.

Conclusions

In this chapter, we have provided a broad ranging definition of HBV and noted that there are a wide range of crime types that may be associated with it, incorporating sex-selective abortions, genital mutilation, forced marriages, and honor killings. HBV appears to be a significant worldwide problem as the prevalence rates for the various forms of it attest. What distinguishes HBV from other forms of violence is that it is often committed with some degree of approval and/or collusion from other family or community members, the offender is typically a family member, there is greater involvement of female family members, and the victims tend to be younger than in other forms of domestic violence. Indeed it is important not to underestimate the importance of honor to some individuals and the lengths family members will go to in order to protect or restore family honor. Frequently, a family will sit down to discuss the issues at hand and the scale of the punishment for the victim.

There is a widely held belief, fueled by Western media coverage, that HBV is a Muslim issue perpetrated especially by Muslims. This is, however, not the case. While HBV involves cultural notions of honor, the violence and the collusion cut across regional, national, and international boundaries. Indeed, HBV, in its many different forms, can be seen in families from Asia, Africa, and Southern Europe, and in some Traveler communities, and it is also seen in Christianity, Judaism, Islam, Sikhism, and Hinduism. Certainly families may use their faith as a defense to HBV practices; however, no recognized religions support HBV.

In the next chapter, we move on to discuss explanatory theories of HBV and try to explain why some individuals feel moved to inflict suffering upon others in the name of honor.

Explanatory Theories of Honor-Based Violence

2

In this chapter, we explore some of the reasons why individuals commit acts of violence in the name of honor. Here we will examine social and psychological factors considered to be important in the motivation of honor-based violence (HBV), how honor-related attitudes, beliefs, and behaviors develop, and how these can foster HBV perpetration.

For professionals, knowledge of the explanatory mechanisms of HBV is likely to be useful in their practice. For example, an understanding of factors that are associated with HBV might help lead to the early identification of HBV cases or allow assessment to be made of the risk posed to potential victims of HBV. Similarly, such an understanding might contribute to the design of community and individual interventions aimed at reducing the occurrence of HBV, issues we will consider in later chapters of this book.

When faced with reports of HBV, many practitioners may have had cause to ask themselves why someone would do this, what could possibly be achieved by inflicting physical and/or psychological pain or even death onto another individual who may be a close relative? The answer to such questions is complex and our understanding of the factors that motivate HBV is in its infancy, but there are some emerging themes that seem especially relevant. Explanations for HBV as they currently exist tend to explain it using a single factor explanation; for example, identifying HBV as a form of male violence against women or as being associated with a particular culture, typically South Asian and Islamic cultures. As we shall see, there are a number of problems with attempting to explain HBV using these single factor explanations. In particular, they are unable to account for all instances of HBV and risk stigmatizing particular cultural and religious groups. Instead, we argue that, for a complete understanding of HBV, theories must consider a number of explanatory factors and consider how these interact with each other in generating motivation.

In this chapter, we, therefore, will review a range of theories that have been used to explain HBV. We will examine the strengths and weaknesses of each theory before drawing together the best aspects of all of the theories into a single multifactor account of HBV. To preempt what is to follow, we will suggest that an explanation of HBV that takes a multilevel approach incorporating social, cultural, and psychological factors can be achieved and may prove particularly useful in our attempts to understand violence of this type (Roberts, 2011).

We begin our discussion by first considering explanations for HBV at the cultural level. We then move on to consider male violence explanations before exploring some psychological models for HBV. Finally, we will attempt to knit together aspects of previous theories to produce a multifactor theory of HBV using the theory of planned behavior (Ajzen, 2011) as the explanatory framework.

Cultural Theories of HBV

In the previous chapter, we noted that honor is a character trait associated with integrity, good moral character, and altruism, and that a sense of honor is an important part of the human condition; honor conceived of in this way is an attractive human quality (Vandello & Cohen, 2003). We also noted another, perhaps more negative definition of honor, centered on the need and ability to "defend" honor. Related to this second definition, there appears to be a number of so-called "honor cultures" throughout the world where honor is central to how the culture defines and organizes itself (Vandello & Cohen, 2003).

Within honor cultures, honor is something that must be maintained and defended. Examples of these honor cultures include Mediterranean societies, such as Greece, Italy, and Spain (Gilmore, 1991); Latin and South American cultures (Johnson & Lipsett-Riverra, 1998); Middle Eastern and Arab cultures (Gilmore, 1990); and the southern United States (Nisbett and Cohen, 1996). In organizing themselves around the concept of honor, honor cultures develop *honor codes* that explicitly stress the importance of obtaining and maintaining honor, and these act as guides to members of the culture regarding acceptable and unacceptable behavior. In the next section, we will explore the characteristics of honor cultures and the extent to which honor codes are implicated in the etiology of HBV.

Honor Cultures

Within honor cultures, codes of honor typically stress the importance of generosity, hospitality, and loyalty (behaviors strongly related to the definition of honor as a character trait), and toughness, sensitivity to insults, and defending reputation and family (behaviors strongly related to the definition of honor as something to be defended (Vandello & Cohen, 2003)). These codes of honor apply to both male and female behavior; however, they place different obligations upon the sexes. Males often have the role of maintaining honor through quickly responding to perceived challenges and insults using their strength, power, and toughness. Males are explicitly encouraged to develop sensitivity to insults and threats to reputation so that they may quickly act to identify and respond to situations where their honor is being challenged. Females, on the other hand, are expected to maintain honor by behaving appropriately through deference, fidelity, modesty, purity, and chastity, and any behaviors that do not conform to this are often stigmatized, explicitly discouraged, and even punished, sometimes violently (Vandello & Cohen, 2003).

To illustrate, honor cultures can be described as stressing "traditional" gender roles in which there is high inequality between the genders. Males have most of the political power and females are expected to maintain subordinate social positions; indeed, females are seen very much as the *responsibility* of the male head of the household (Vandello & Cohen, 2003). This means that the behavior of females not only reflects upon their own honor, but also has a powerful impact upon the honor of males. As such, another important element of male honor is the behavior and reputation of females for whom the male has responsibility. A man, therefore, can be dishonored, not only by insults and challenges directed toward him by others, but by the behavior of females. It is particularly noteworthy that within honor cultures a man's ability to protect and control females is seen as a proxy for the extent to which he also is able to protect his honor in other spheres. Should a man be seen to be unable to control a female (if she contravenes one of the social strictures for female behavior), this will be interpreted as a sign that the man is vulnerable and weak and someone who can be taken advantage of in other situations (Pitt-Rivers, 1966). Female sexual behavior is of particular concern to males and, in many honor cultures, dishonor is felt by males even in circumstances where female family members have been victims of crimes, such as rape and sexual assault (Johal, 2003; note also the response to and use of rape in HBV described in Chapter 1). Ultimately, in honor cultures, the costs of female behavior are felt acutely by males and have implications across all of a man's interactions with others.

Within an honor culture, in order to "protect" against dishonor by female behavior, males have a need to manage female behavior. As such, males frequently use strategies to "protect" and "defend" females from dishonor that effectively limit female freedom. Strategies of tight behavioral control, monitoring, and punishment for transgression are common. For example, males may limit the possibilities for females to engage with others in a work or social context by determining if a female can work, the types of work she should carry out, if and with whom she is allowed to associate and develop friendships, set limits on self-expression (such as determining appropriate dress and social behavior), and set strict guidelines upon the types of interaction females may have with males including who they may develop relationships with and the opportunity to question decisions made by a male patriarch. These controls should be compared with the characteristic behaviors of HBV described in Chapter 1; many of the HBV behaviors are strongly characteristic of attempts made by males to exert control over females and the punishment that results for transgression. This male preoccupation with female behavior, use of violence to punish transgressions of honor codes, and a general acceptability of violence within honor cultures has been implicated in an observed high incidence of violence against women within these cultures compared to others (Vandello & Cohen, 2003; Anderson, 1994).

Being seen by others to have *honor* is very important within an honor culture and loss of honor can be very damaging both socially and psychologically (Vandello & Cohen, 2003). Certainly, loss of honor may mark a family as being undesirable or untrustworthy and thus stigmatizing them. Likewise, an individual who loses honor may feel an acute sense of shame and exposure in front of others (see section Honor, Shame, and Violence concerning the role of shame in HBV). To avoid this, a family's public compliance with codes of honor is crucial. Indeed, public compliance with the rules contained within codes of honor may be used as a means of demonstrating that a family has honor to others outside the family. By this account, behavior associated with HBV, such as forced marriage, genital mutilation, and honor killings, may be viewed both as attempts to regain honor where honor has been lost and a public demonstration that a family has honor (Vandello & Cohen, 2003). In support of this idea, it is notable that many individuals, when brought to account for suspected HBV, enact defenses claiming their actions were motivated out of sensitivity to cultural norms and practices (Smartt, 2006). We have already mentioned that it is important not to underestimate the power of cultural norms and the importance some individuals attach to them. Should an individual be part of an honor culture, their continued membership in the culture may rest on being seen to accept and behave in accordance with dominant cultural norms. While not a valid excuse for HBV, the extent to which an individual accepts these cultural norms perhaps provides a partial explanation for its attraction to some individuals.

The importance of honor is aptly illustrated by the quotation below from Sirhan, aged 35, who was interviewed for an ABC documentary, *The Lost Honor of Sirhan*. He was interviewed having completed a six-month prison sentence in Jordan for killing his sister, who was a victim of rape:

> I would rather die than lose my honor. ... Our whole life is founded on honor. If we lose it, we have no life, we become swine. If we lose our honor, we are just like swine. We're no better than animals.

Within honor cultures, it is important to note that females do have some, albeit limited, power and, therefore, are not completely passive. Females can be said to have *negative power* such that they may stain the reputation of the family by their acts, and considerable *positive power* such that they may act to increase the reputation and status of the family by marrying someone of higher social status and also by helping ensure compliance of others with a male's and/or the family's wishes (Schneider, 1971). In this regard, it is interesting that an aspect of HBV that seems to distinguish it from other forms of domestic violence (which generally involve males acting alone against other family members) is that female family members are often directly involved in the violence, either as active participants, or in the planning and encouragement of it (Smartt, 2006).

The attitudes and beliefs of some women that may be supportive of honor themes was illustrated in work carried out by the British charity Karma Nirvana (2004) that works with victims of HBV. They asked a group of South Asian women, aged 25 to 57 in the United Kingdom, if they had a choice between honor and their daughter, what would they choose. The women unanimously chose honor.

The behavior of subordinate males, such as young men, is also of high significance within honor cultures. They, like females, should behave in a respectful manner and take heed of the wishes of more senior, usually older, males. The behavior of subordinate males can dishonor others in a number of ways; through disrespect of an elder, for example, but perhaps more relevant to HBV is their behavior toward females, especially those they chose as dating or sexual partners. As we have seen, protecting the fidelity of daughters is very important in honor cultures and parental control over a daughter's choice of partner, a requirement to seek the blessing of family prior to dating, and a ban on any form of intimacy prior to marriage is often highly important. Behavior that infringes these requirements is by definition dishonoring of the girl's family, especially her father. The senior male will be required to use strategies to maintain and regain control over the subordinate male as well as his female family members including the use of violence (Abu-Lughod, 2011). The relevance of this to HBV is that, as we saw in Chapter 1, while females are the most likely victims of HBV, there is a small, albeit significant, incidence of male victimization, and HBV against males is most often carried out by family members who disapprove of the relationship between a female family member and the male, or due to the sexuality of a male family member (Chesler, 2010).

It is important to note that this explanation of HBV relating it, in part, to honor cultures is not equivalent to blaming particular nationalities or religions for HBV as many media accounts have done (Meetoo & Mirza, 2007). Certainly, blaming HBV on particular nationalities or religious groups is unhelpful as it unduly stigmatizes these groups and does little to inform treatment or management of victims or offenders (Abu-Lughod, 2011). Instead, the honor culture explanation stresses that HBV is more likely within cultures that put a high value on the maintenance of honor. As such,

HBV is possible in any geographical area and can be perpetrated by members of any religion as prevalence studies have demonstrated (Chesler, 2010). Most cultures are sensitive to the behavior of young males and females and many parents are concerned about their children's relationship choice. The distinction is, of course, the degree of importance that is placed upon honor within a culture. Similarly, it is entirely possible for individuals from non-honor cultures to develop honor codes of their own and behave accordingly. It also is important to stress that honor within cultures has positive as well as negative effects. Honor codes act as an effective form of social control, maintaining social hierarchies, morals, and relationships between members of the culture, and many members of a culture will voluntarily strive to maintain honor for themselves and their family (Abu-Lughod, 2011).

To summarize, honor appears to be an important feature of the human condition valued by many cultures. It is significantly more important in some cultures where notions of honor become central to the maintenance of social order, and these have been described as honor cultures. Having honor is particularly important for males and an inability to maintain and defend honor is often seen as weakness. The genders differ with respect to their responsibilities in the maintenance of honor; males are required to be active and maintain honor using, when necessary, force, whereas females are required to maintain honor by avoiding prescribed behaviors and adopting deference to the male family head. Honor appears to be particularly located within female behavior and males are judged by their ability to maintain control over females. Where female (and at times male) behavior transgresses social strictures, males and other family members are required to regain honor by demonstrating their control and dominance over the errant female (or subordinate male). HBV, therefore, may be seen in part as motivated by a need to demonstrate that a family has honor, as much as these acts also may be about maintaining or regaining honor. Within this formulation, acts, such as forced marriage, genital mutilation, and honor killings, may be acts designed to publicly demonstrate that honor resides within a family. We now move on to explore how honor cultures arise, how honor codes are transmitted throughout a culture, and how these impact upon and become internalized by individuals.

The Evolution of Honor Cultures

Cultural codes are effectively social rules that stress expected ways of behaving and incorporate a series of cultural norms. Cultural norms are sets of attitudes and beliefs that give explanations and cultural meanings to behaviors. Cultural norms describe ways of behaving that are expected and promoted by a culture and they evolve from behavioral responses to the environment in which individuals live. Generally those behaviors that are promoted, sustained, and become part of cultural norms are those that are useful to the survival of a group. Such behaviors might include cooperation with other members of the group in hunting or collecting food, or protecting one's offspring from attack. However, not all behavioral responses to the environment become part of a set of cultural norms. Behaviors less useful to survival may be discouraged and so are likely to diminish and not become part of cultural norms. Behaviors, such as attacking and stealing from members of one's own group or neglect of one's offspring, are examples of these (Vandello & Cohen, 2003). Interestingly, many acts that are regarded as proscribed activities within common law, such as murder, child neglect, and theft, can be seen to be acts that in evolutionary terms do not enhance the survival of a social group.

This account of the development of cultural norms has been applied to the development of cultures of honor. Cultures of honor seem particularly to have developed within frontier lands, such as deserts or other harsh environments, where survival was difficult, state governments often weak, and law enforcement limited, if not nonexistent. Indeed, many of these conditions pertain today in areas where honor violence is prevalent, e.g., tribal areas of West Pakistan, rural India, and rural parts of Western Turkey.

Historically, in these frontier environments, competition between individuals for scarce resources often led to threats of and actual violence between individuals. As a result, in order to survive the ability to fend for and protect oneself and family was of fundamental importance (Schneider, 1971). Reputation was also an important element of protecting oneself and family as it acted as deterrence to would-be attackers and reduced the likelihood of future attacks. To create a reputation, individuals, especially males, had to let others know that even on small matters they were not to be trifled with and that they were willing and able to use extreme measures, including violence, to defend what was theirs. Failure to do this led to a reputation for weakness and left them more vulnerable to attack (Schneider, 1971). Hence, an individual's reputation became an important currency.

In frontier areas, economies based upon animal husbandry and herding were also common (Fischer, 1989), and caring for and protecting livestock also facilitated and encouraged the development of vigilance and the use of aggression (Schneider, 1971). Behaviors, such as toughness and an ability to recognize and deal with threats quickly, were likely to be useful survival strategies for individuals in these contexts and, as they also promoted survival, they became socially valued and expected behaviors. Ultimately, an individual's honor became associated with his reputation and the extent to which he behaved in accordance with these valued cultural norms (Cohen, 1998; Cohen, Vandello, & Rantilla, 1998; Cohen, Vandello, Puente, & Rantilla, 1999).

To summarize, honor-related cultural norms developed out of a need to protect one's kin and resources. Honor became the byword for reputation and something to be defended and maintained, and violence became an acceptable way of doing this. An important question to consider now is how cultures of honor continue, especially given that in much of the world the environmental conditions that gave rise to such cultural norms do not exist today.

Maintenance of Honor Codes

As cultural norms develop, they become explicitly and implicitly reinforced. This happens through socialization of children and reinforcement within a community through such things as religion and inclusion in law and policy (Cohen, 1998). Over time, cultural norms become internalized by individuals as behavioral scripts that may never be consciously considered or questioned by individuals and, even if they are questioned, rarely refuted (Vandello & Cohen, 2004; Triandis, 1994). The cultural norms may ultimately become so ingrained into the behavioral scripts of individual members of a cultural group that they become part of the culture's sense of identity, i.e., *who* they are. (We shall explore identity later in this chapter.) Individuals effectively grow up in a context in which the cultural norms dominated, defining the group to themselves and outsiders. Cultural norms of this kind are highly resistant to change because any challenge to a norm is not just a challenge to the norm itself, but to the very essence of the culture's sense of itself, how it sees itself, and what it stands for. Cultural norms, therefore, place significant demands upon individuals to behave in accordance with them and transgressions from them may be met with a variety of social sanctions. Undeniably, for many individuals it is easier simply not to question the norm than to run the risk of challenging the nature of the culture of which they are a member (Breakwell, 1982).

So far, we have explored the nature of honor and the characteristics of honor-related norms. We also have explored how honor cultures evolve and how honor norms persist over time, sometimes long after their environmental usefulness has gone. We now move on to consider to what extent holding honor norms is sufficient and necessary for honor-based violence to occur.

Honor Norms and HBV

Vandello and Cohen (2003) argue that violence is likely in honor cultures that stress toughness, respect, and protection of one's own kin, and have noted that there is a higher incidence of various forms of domestic violence within cultures that stress honor than in other comparable cultures. In related work, Gill (2004) reports that low-violence cultures are those that have strong sanctions against interpersonal violence, in which females have power outside of the home, where notions of masculinity are not directly linked to male dominance and honor, and there is equality in decision making and resource allocation within the family. These qualities are frequently absent in honor cultures. This suggests that honor norms and values have some relationship to various forms of violence, both domestic violence and violence outside families. It is likely that these honor norms have their effects by setting cultural expectations about the acceptability of violence as a solution to actual or perceived loses of honor. Where concerns center on losses of honor and where violence is more acceptable as a problem-solving tool, violence is more likely to occur. As many honor concerns center around family issues, domestic violence rates will be higher in honor cultures. Similarly, as honor is related as well to male status concerns, the rates of male-on-male violence will be higher in honor cultures than in other cultures (Cohen, Vandello, & Rantilla, 1998).

While the risk of violence is increased within an honor culture, violence is not inevitable. Cultural norms might be supportive of violent solutions to challenges to honor; however, it is ultimately the individual who must, at some level, make a decision whether or not to act in accordance with these norms. Hence, being part of an honor culture does not in itself guarantee that an individual will respond with violence to a threat to his honor. Without a doubt, there are many potential reasons why an individual would not use violence even in the face of threats to his honor. For example, an individual may fear prosecution, he may not personally subscribe to honor related themes, or he may reject violence as a solution.

Given this explanation for honor-based violence that suggests it is solely a result of honor norms or an honor culture is too simplistic and, as we have noted, does risk stigmatizing certain communities and cultures. A full explanation for HBV, therefore, must include other factors, in particular, how cultural norms and challenges to honor affect individuals and how this leads, in some cases, to violence. In further developing an explanation for HBV, we will explore how culture might influence attitudes and beliefs and how these may, along with other factors, such as beliefs about the opinions of others and opportunity to act, may give rise to HBV.

HBV as Male Violence

Another theoretical account for HBV sees it as a form of gendered violence, specifically, a form of violence against women perpetrated by men. Within this approach, HBV is a consequence of male attempts to maintain power and control over women (Meetoo & Miraz, 2007). The data on HBV incidents lends some support to this view as most perpetrators of HBV are males and most victims are females (Chesler, 2010). Similarly, HBV appears to be important in maintaining control over and to punish perceived wrongdoing by female family members.

This account of HBV is important as it attempts to demystify HBV by stressing its similarity to other forms of gendered violence. It acts as a challenge to views of HBV that attempt to locate it within particular (usually Islamic, Arab, Kurdish, and South Asian) cultures that are prevalent in the media and are ultimately unhelpful because, as stated above, they result in stigmatizing certain groups. Finally, it allows practitioners and activists to draw upon approaches to challenging the behavior that have been useful in the broader field of domestic violence.

However, there is research that presents a strong challenge to this account. Research has demonstrated that males are also victims of HBV and there are cases of female perpetration of HBV, either as instigators, planners, or even involvement in the violence (Chesler, 2010). Another problem with this account of HBV is that, in focusing exclusively upon women as victims of HBV, it runs the risk of ignoring male victims who, while a minority, also suffer abuse.

While it is acknowledged that many of the cultural or honor-based norms that support HBV perpetration are concerned with the control and domination of women (in particular, the idea that women's lives, their opportunities, and fidelity has to be controlled by men) and are precisely the norms that are supportive of domestic violence, in general. However, it seems that the male violence account of HBV falls short in offering a complete explanation for all incidences of HBV; in particular, it does not explain why some males are victims and some females are perpetrators. HBV, therefore, is not simply concerned with male-perpetrated violence against and dominance over women. Instead, HBV appears to be more a reflection of broader issues of social control and systems of power (Walby, 1990) in which males are responsible for controlling both females and weaker males in the service of honor. If HBV is conceived of in this way, it is interesting that the male violence account of HBV is consistent with an honor culture view of HBV as both models stress how defined gender roles and control over women give tacit justification for violent action. Certainly, as we have seen, honor cultures often have explicit norms that require different behavior of the genders and explicitly encourage male dominance and control over women (Vandello & Cohen, 2003).

The male violence model identifies attitudes and beliefs that may serve to legitimize and offer tacit support and even encouragement for HBV. However, as we have noted earlier, holding on to attitudes and beliefs that are supportive of HBV does not necessarily guarantee that an individual would act in this way. In fact, perhaps the best that can be said when applying both the cultural and gendered violence models of HBV is that, in order to carry out HBV, an individual would be likely to have internalized attitudes and beliefs that support violent subjugation of both females and males in the service of honor.

The honor culture and male violence models considered thus far suggest an inevitability of HBV, such that cultures with gendered and honor-based norms should give rise to this type of violence. However, as stated previously, it is important to consider the impact of these cultural norms upon the individual and the processes that lead some individuals to act violently while others do not. In order to consider this, we move on to explore psychologically oriented accounts of HBV. We begin by exploring identity theory and how an individual's sense of identity may develop and influence his/her behavior.

Psychological Models of HBV

Identity and HBV

As we have seen, cultural norms (and indeed any set of attitudes and beliefs) can be explicitly and implicitly reinforced through processes of socialization and can become internalized by individuals. However, cultural norms are internalized to different degrees depending upon the individuals concerned. The extent to which cultural norms are internalized depends upon a multitude of factors including the socialization an individual experiences, i.e., what norms and values were reinforced by the parents and by society itself; an individual's exposure to other cultural norms, attitude, and belief systems that differ from those of his/her own culture; and the motivation of the individual to accept the cultural norms (Stets & Burke, 2000).

Some individuals will internalize cultural norms to the extent that they become part of their sense of self, who they are, or, put another way, their identity. For others, cultural norms may be internalized to a lesser extent and will have a more limited impact upon their identity, and for some individuals, they may not be internalized at all. In examining the impact of culture upon individuals, identity theory (Stets & Burke, 2000) provides an interesting theoretical structure that links the social world of cultural norms to the behavior of the individual. In particular, identity theory may be used to explain how cultural norms become incorporated into an individual's sense of self—his/her identity—and aspects of this theory can be used to account for differences in the importance of cultural norms between individuals.

An identity can be considered to be the set of meanings that define who an individual is; their sense of self (Burke, 2003). An individual's identity is made up of a combination of different subidentities that are related to the groups (*group identities*), roles (*role identities*), and personal characteristics (*personal identities*) an individual has. *Group identities* are identities that relate to the groups or classifications that an individual believes he/she belongs (for example, British, male, female), *role identities* relate to the roles that an individual plays in his/her day-to-day life (for example, lawyer, mother, father), and *personal identities* or *personal attributes* relate to particular characteristics that an individual believes he/she has (for example, sociable, honorable, honest). These different identities are idiosyncratic and relate to what individuals believe about themselves; as such, they may be subject to bias and inaccuracy. For example, the role identity of "mother" includes what it means to a particular individual to be a mother; this may include notions of nurturance and care of children, love, and support. Another individual also might share the role identity of "mother;" however, her conception might differ significantly, perhaps involving a rejection of nurturance and stressing independence of children.

Identities cover the full range of activities an individual may be involved in throughout his/her life. Identities develop over time and are based on an individual's experience. Socialization processes and life experiences, therefore, are significant in the development of different identities (Burke, 2003; Stets and Burke, 2000).

The meanings contained within an individual's various identities contain standards that are used for assessing the meaning of situations to individuals. These meanings also detail what behavior they should exhibit within a situation and how others ought to behave. These are referred to as *identity standards* and are used by individuals to interpret situations and to guide their behavior. In any situation, an individual will extract various meanings from such things as the behavior of others and other environmental cues that are personally relevant, and will compare these with the standards contained within his/her identity. Any differences between an individual's identity standards and the actual situation (for example, where an individual fails to behave in accordance with the expectations of a cultural norm important to the observer) will give rise to a perception of *error*, a mismatch between what is expected and what is actually occurring. Where the mismatch between the actual and expected meanings in a situation is large or increasing, individuals generally experience negative emotions and will generally act to change the situation in the direction of what is expected. Where there is a small or decreasing discrepancy, individuals generally do not change their behavior (Burke, 1991). So, for example, an individual holding the role identity "mother" might hold meanings, such as protect, nurture, and care for children. When in a situation involving children, the "mother" identity will be used to interpret the situation and inform the individual what behavior she should enact. It also will be used to judge the behavior of others in terms of how it conforms to the "mother" identity. Where another individual is neglectful of a child, i.e., where the behavioral standard for mother and the relevant expectations have been compromised, the mismatch between the expectations and the standards contained in the "mother" identity will instigate negative emotions and this may lead to action to change the situation (the individual might intervene to protect the child) to what is expected. Identities effectively help individuals make sense of their world, informing them of what factors are relevant in any situation and how to deal with the situation.

Identities differ in terms of their relative importance. The most important or salient identities will strongly influence an individual's behavior across a wide range of situations because they will lead an individual to judge most situations in the light of those salient identities (Stets & Burke, 2000). Hence, if a particular identity is important to an individual, he/she will tend to judge most situations, including his/her own behavior and the behavior of others, with respect to the behavioral standards contained within the identity.

The presence of different identities means also that some identities will be incompatible with each other, i.e., some identities contain meanings that are difficult to reconcile (Stets & Burke, 2000). For example, some of the meanings associated with being a "police officer," such as carrying a gun, working shifts, and wearing a uniform, may be incompatible with an identity such as being a "mother" requiring care, nurturance, and being available for a child. In different situations, different identities might be salient. For example, being at home with a child, the mother identity is likely to be salient, where as being at work, the police officer identity is likely to be salient.

When important identities are salient at different times, they are likely to be much easier to reconcile than where different identities are salient and place demands on an individual at the same time. For example, a report about a police officer's child being sick while she is at work may enact the "mother" role identity calling for care and nurturance of the child, which may be incompatible with the role identity "police officer" and may interfere with her capacity to perform the role of police officer. In cases of competing identities, individuals must appraise the situation and form judgments related to the most appropriate meanings in the situation to which they should respond. This will be guided by the relative importance of their identities with the most important identities taking precedence (Stryker & Burke, 2000). Of course, where identities are of similar importance, this may present the individual with a dilemma. Experiencing incompatible identities that are of similar importance is a stressful experience and individuals often respond to this by attempting to modify one of their identities, e.g., a father may cease working shifts, or they may reject that identity, e.g., a father may leave work entirely to be with his child. However, some identities are of such importance to an individual that they will not be rejected or modified.

Finally, the number of identities an individual has is significant. Where individuals have a few very important identities, their entire being may become dominated by these. In this case, individuals might judge most situations against and behave in accordance with the particular identity most of the time. Behaving consistently with the meanings of the identity then becomes the dominant behavior pattern for the individual. For example, an individual who has "police officer" as the single most important identity, even when not working, may behave and judge situations with respect to this single identity. Also, individuals with few identities are less likely to experience discomfort due to incompatible identities. Definitely, one of the reasons for rejecting identities is to minimize the occurrence of this (Stets & Burke, 2000).

Thus, an individual's behavior is strongly related to the contents of his/her identities and the relative importance of them. Mismatches between expected meanings in a situation and actual meanings serve to motivate action to respond to the mismatches. Essentially, identities bias judgments in favor of salient identities and compel behavior that is consistent with them.

Applying this theory to HBV, socialization throughout the lifespan will influence the development and contents of different identities. The extent to which an individual has internalized honor codes will influence the extent his/her identities contain meanings that are supportive of honor and by association HBV. This, in turn, will influence his/her judgments of situations and, ultimately, the likelihood of carrying out an act of HBV. Identities that contain meanings stressing the importance of maintaining honor, honor-related gender roles, and an acceptance of violence as a solution to dishonor are those that would be expected to be most associated with HBV.

Where an individual's salient identities are strongly associated with honor codes, an individual will be biased to judge situations in terms of honor-related expectations. This means that in interpreting many situations, meanings will be judged against an honor-related standard and, where honor-related meanings are not present, negative emotion is likely to result. The behaviors that honor identities would require an individual to enact would be those designed to create, restore, or maintain honor. Individuals whose identities were supportive of the use of violence would be most likely to enact violence in the pursuit of honor.

In the case of competing identities, this may illustrate one of the reasons why not everyone who grows up within an honor culture would engage in HBV. Some identities, such as a strong identity related to parenthood, likely featuring meanings of nurturance and support for a child, would act in direct contrast and opposition to honor-related identities that were supportive of HBV. In a situation where honor norms suggest violence toward a family member to preserve honor, the parental identity may then compete with honor identities. Where the parental identity was particularly strong, some individuals may choose to cope with this by selecting the parental identity and so would be unlikely to carry out an act of HBV because of the damage it may do to their child. Conversely other individuals may act on the honor identities and may commit HBV. This also may help explain an observation that some perpetrators, especially family members, while feeling vindicated, are simultaneously very distressed at having carried out an act of HBV; perhaps these individuals are struggling to reconcile their parental identity with having acted on an honor identity. The honor identity supports the violence and the meanings associated with violence; however, the parental identity is inconsistent with the violent meanings and the mismatch will produce emotion designed to impel parental behavior. Logically, this situation may operate in reverse such that an individual with parental and honor identities, who doesn't act to restore honor, also may feel strong emotion because his/her honor identity compels him/her to act to restore honor.

It is important to note when discussing identities that we are referring to fundamental constructs that define how individuals see themselves. Indeed the extent to which individuals are able to create acceptable identities and behave in ways that are consistent with them is closely tied to an individual's sense of self-worth, their self-esteem (Breakwell, 1982). As such, for individuals with salient honor-related identities, a lack of honor (a mismatch between the identity standard and the situation) is a direct threat to their identity and ultimately their self-esteem. As such, carrying out an act of HBV is not simply acting to maintain cultural norms or to restore honor for honor's sake. Rather, for some individuals, HBV is about acting to preserve and defend their sense of self-worth.

Applying identity theory to HBV helps to explain some key aspects of HBV. To begin, the model is gender neutral and so does not preclude male or female perpetration of HBV. Similarly, it can be used to show how internalized cultural norms can influence behavior acting as a lens through which situations are judged. The model also allows a deeper understanding of the psychological states that motivate HBV, i.e., for some individuals, HBV is a means of defending not just honor but their own sense of self and self-worth. The notion of competing identities also may help explain why not all individuals from an honor culture would carry out HBV. Identities do not, a priori, have to contain meanings that are obtained from a dominant culture. Meanings can be generated from any source including personal experience, reading books and documents, etc. Given this, it is worth also noting that the identity model does not preclude individuals who are not part of an honor culture committing acts of HBV.

The identity model, however, is limited as a full explanation of HBV. The model requires the creation of identities that are supportive of HBV. What is not clear is exactly what meanings HBV or honor-related identities would contain. It is possible to speculate that the meanings would be related to honor-based cultural norms; however, no research to date has explored this. It also is not clear if all perpetrators of HBV hold honor-related identities and act in accordance with them. This may be the case; however, no research has thus far been carried out to test this hypothesis. In fact, it may be very difficult to empirically demonstrate that all perpetrators of HBV have internalized HBV norms as that research would necessarily rest upon self-report that is subject to various biases including social desirability responding of participants. Research also needs to explore the extent to which other competing identities interact with honor-related identities. The model also does not consider the beliefs an individual has about the attitudes of others. This has been shown to be significant in determining whether an individual will act, such that where an individual believes that there is a high consensus in favor of carrying out a particular act, he/she is more likely to act (Ajzen, 2011). Given this, this explanation for honor-based violence represents an intriguing model, but one that requires further empirical exploration.

Relevant to HBV, it is interesting to explore exactly what emotions might be enacted where there is a mismatch between salient identity standards and the situation. Threats to identities and self-esteem give rise to significant discomfort in individuals and emotions, such as shame, anxiety, and anger are common (Breakwell, 1982). If mismatches are considered as threats of this kind, then a lack of honor may for some individuals be associated with these emotions. In fact, research has demonstrated that loss of honor or challenges to honor result specifically in the experience of shame (Gilbert, 1998). In the next section we now move on to explore the impact of shame upon behavior and the relevance of this to HBV.

Honor, Shame, and Violence

Honor-based violence has often been associated with the experience of shame and some have argued that shame is strongly associated with, if not a motivator of, HBV (Coomaraswamy, 2005). Shame is a powerful emotion that appears to be induced by an individual's awareness of dishonor, disgrace, or condemnation. Shame consists of painful feelings about the self, uncomfortable emotional arousal, acute discomfort, and the feeling of being exposed (Fossum & Mason, 1986; Gilbert, 1998). As shame is a negative emotional state, individuals are motivated to minimize feelings of shame and will behave in ways designed to avoid or remove the source of shame (Gilbert, 1998). Shame can be self-generated, such as feeling ashamed of one's actions, or by the behavior of others. Shaming acts by others can include verbal and physical attacks on the personal dignity of an individual or group, ridicule and name calling, and exposing an individual's or group's vulnerabilities or weaknesses.

Crucial to the experience of shame generated by the behavior of others is an individual's perception of the behavior. Observing behavior that transgresses important cultural norms can be an acutely shaming experience both for the transgressor and for the observer (Gilbert, 1998). Indeed, as we saw above, where an individual holds honor-based identities, he/she will judge many situations against the identity honor standard and mismatches are perceived as a challenge to the identity. Hence, as regards carrying out various forms of HBV, such as honor killings or beatings in response to perceived transgressions of cultural norms or honor identity standards, a strong motivation to act and be seen by others to act is the need to remove the source of the shame and reduce the negative shame experience.

Relevant also to explaining HBV is an association between the experience of shame and expressions of extreme anger or rage (Tangney et al., 1996). For some individuals, the experience of shame provokes uncontrolled rage that often results in violent attacks upon the source of the shame. This is interesting when one considers honor killings or related violent assaults. In some circumstances, the attacks can be sudden and extremely violent with victims suffering many injuries. It, therefore, may be that attacks of this kind are illustrative of an acute shame reaction leading to rage-motivated violence on the part of the offender. Research has so far not explored this; however, data is suggestive of this as a possible explanation for some of the more violent attacks upon victims.

The association between the experience of shame, shame-rage, and some types of HBV appear to explain a possible psychological state when the intention of the HBV is to remove negative emotions associated with a behavioral transgression. However, as well as carrying out HBV as a response to being shamed as may be the case with honor killings, individuals also carry out HBV because they wish to *avoid* the experience of being shamed, i.e., genital mutilation and forced marriage may be carried out to comply with cultural norms to avoid the experience of shame caused by failing to act (this also may be an aspect of the motivation for responsive acts such as honor killings).

The actual experience of shame, therefore, may not be sufficient to explain all cases of HBV. Fear of shame or shame avoidance may be an important element in motivation as well. Here individuals do not experience shame, per se, but anxiety in response to the risk of experiencing shame. Anxiety then acts as an emotional motivator to act. As such, it is too simplistic to posit the experience of shame as the sole psychological motivation for HBV. Instead, we need to consider the involvement of other psychological and social factors. For example, as we have seen, shame may be the emotional response, but individuals need to have internalized attitudes and beliefs that impel them to judge situations against honor-based criteria before they can experience shame in a situation.

So far, we have considered a number of explanations for HBV and each one has some strengths and weaknesses. It is likely, therefore, as with many other social phenomena, that a single factor explanation for HBV is not possible. Instead, as we have suggested above, a multifactor model of HBV is most parsimonious with what is currently know about HBV, and we will begin to explore such an approach in the remainder of the chapter. We begin by considering the role of the environment or situation upon HBV.

The Role of the Environment/Situation

In explaining HBV, another important factor that any model must consider is the environment/situation in which an individual finds him or herself. The situation is crucial to behavior as it can increase the likelihood of certain acts or decrease the likelihood of others with the (non) availability of resources and opportunity to behave (Mischel, 1992). This is not trivial because, if we are attempting to explain HBV, we need to consider the role of those environmental/situational factors that serve to increase or reduce its likelihood. While psychological and social conditions may be supportive of an act of HBV, the situation may not be, as there may be police or other potential witnesses present or the intended victim may be unavailable.

All of the models considered so far give limited consideration to the role of the situation. The honor culture and male violence models do not explicitly consider situational factors at all, while the identity model does allow for individual appraisal of situations and the meanings they hold. However, a full model of HBV should be able to account for the impact of social, psychological, and situational factors on behavior.

In the next section, we move on to consider a model that is able to do this by knitting together the various explanations for HBV considered thus far. The model is not a model of HBV per se, but a more general model of behavior that can be applied to HBV. The model is referred to as the Theory of Planned Behavior (Ajzen, 2011) and explicitly links together psychological, social, and environmental factors in explaining behavior.

Theory of Planned Behavior and HBV

So far, we have considered social explanations, such as culture and gender, identity- and emotion-related explanations for HBV. In this section, we attempt to knit these explanations together into a multifactor model that explains HBV and leads to the generation of testable hypotheses for future research. In considering how these various explanations might be linked together within an empirically validated theoretical structure, the theory of planned behavior (TPB) (Ajzen, 2012) forms a useful explanatory framework.

The theory of planned behavior suggests that human behavior is guided by three important elements. These include:

- *Behavioral beliefs:* Beliefs about and evaluation of the likely outcome of a particular behavior

- *Normative beliefs:* Beliefs about the normative expectations of other individuals (what one believes others would expect one to do in an analogous situation)
- *Control beliefs:* Beliefs about various factors and their respective strength that facilitate or impede the performance of the behavior.

Behavioral beliefs impact upon an individual's *attitude* toward a particular behavior that can be favorable or unfavorable.

Normative beliefs influence the degree of social pressure an individual feels there is to behave in a particular manner; this is referred to as the *subjective norm* where high perceived social pressure is related to a subjective norm that the behavior is desirable, whereas low perceived social pressure leads to a subjective norm that the behavior is undesirable. Control beliefs give rise to *perceived behavioral control*, the extent to which an individual believes that the behavior is within his/her control to perform.

An individual's *attitude* to a behavior, the *subjective norm* associated with the behavior, and the *perceived behavioral control* combine to give rise to an *intention* to perform or not to perform the behavior. Generally, the intention to perform the behavior will be high if the attitude an individual has toward performing it is positive, if the subjective norm concerning the behavior is supportive, and if the individual perceives high behavioral control to carry out the behavior. *Actual behavioral control* is the extent to which an individual is, in reality, able to perform the behavior and rests upon factors such as the degree to which the environment/situation facilitates or impedes the behavior. Hence, given a strong enough behavioral intention and sufficient actual behavioral control, individuals will carry out the behavior if an opportunity arises to do so.

The theoretical approaches discussed earlier can be combined into the theory of planned behavior framework to suggest a multifactor model for HBV. As detailed earlier, honor cultures stress roles for males and females and their expected behaviors. They also stress the importance of defending honor and acceptable ways of achieving this. Socialization of individuals effectively describes the culturally important standards and behaviors and this includes the tacit message that these are expected. Social support and even rewards come from behaving in accordance with the cultural norms; this can be in the form of praise for the behavior and acceptance as part of the community. Failure to behave in accordance with the cultural norms can result in criticism, social ostracism, and even punishment. The impact of socialization is internalization of cultural norms, which, as we have seen, can form part of group, role, and personal identities. Identities in turn will inform beliefs and attitudes impacting upon interpretations and expectations of situations.

Within the TPB, it becomes possible to identify those conditions where HBV would be more likely. Internalization of honor-related cultural norms and subsequent development of honor-related identities is likely to result in individuals developing *behavioral beliefs* that stress the importance of honor, reputation, and toughness and *attitudes* in favor of behaviors (use of violence, threats, and control strategies) that achieve this. Individuals will use their identity meanings to interpret situations, and should the behavior mismatch with that expected, for example, should an individual transgress honor-related cultural norms, emotion, in particular shame, arises that impels a need for action in response.

In an honor culture, honor is a centrally important driver that defines many aspects of the culture. For an individual living within that culture, a reasonable assumption would be that other people from the culture would share the view that honor is important and of the acceptable ways of obtaining and maintaining it, including the use of violence. As such, individuals are likely to believe that others would support HBV. Therefore, this belief is likely to inform their *subjective norm* favoring violent solutions in response to challenges to honor.

Given honor-related identities, resultant beliefs and attitudes favoring HBV, and a favorable subjective norm for HBV, the only caveats to violence actually occurring are the *perceived* and *actual behavioral control* related to HBV that an individual has. This is where the model considers the role of the environment/situation to support or curtail behavior. Within an honor culture, there may be factors that serve to increase perceived and actual behavioral control making HBV more likely (e.g., individuals may have been socialized to perceive that they have the capability to carry out a violent act when honor is threatened), there may be few if any sanctions against HBV, and/or there may be structural support that facilitates carrying out HBV, including active help from other individuals.

Of course, the opportunity to carry out an act of HBV also must be available even if all of the other conditions are in place, and this rests upon the availability of the victim and the means with which to affect an attack. This model accounts for the research data. It is gender neutral and so can account for male and female perpetration and victimization. Likewise, it accounts for the observation that HBV can occur in different countries and is not located within specific religions or nationalities.

As well as suggesting the conditions that need be in place for HBV to occur, the TPB also can shed some light on why HBV does not occur, even in circumstances where individuals who are part of an honor culture may be dishonored. Some individuals may not internalize honor cultural norms, thus failing to develop beliefs and attitudes that favor HBV. They also may develop competing identities that stress the importance of other behaviors opposed to HBV. This may happen for any number of reasons, because they have internalized different cultural messages either through being part of a culture or subculture that stresses nonviolent behavior, poor or different (nonhonor-based) socialization from parents, or they may have come to unilaterally question and reject the norms perhaps through exposure to other cultures.

The strength of a subjective norm also will vary dependent upon the strength of the perceived social consensus toward acting. So, should an individual be aware of a developing consensus against acting, this may challenge the belief that others would carry out HBV. This may be the case where an individual lives in an environment where the dominant culture is opposed to HBV. This is noteworthy considering some of the interventions that we will describe in later chapters of this book. In all of these circumstances, the intention to act may become attenuated, thus making behavior less likely.

Conclusion

As we stated at the start of this chapter, the explanatory literature on HBV is in its infancy and limited empirical research has been conducted that seeks to test out explanatory models. In this chapter, we have explored various explanations for HBV and noted that each of them, for various reasons, has not provided a full explanation. Honor culture and male violence models have explained some of the social and structural contexts, the values and norms that are important in the development of HBV. However, culture models fail to fully account for individual differences in perpetration and male violence models fail to fully account for male victimization and female perpetration. We explored identity theory and applied this to HBV noting how cultural messages favoring honor can become internalized through socialization and incorporated into identities and, ultimately, into an individual's sense of self. We saw how individuals judge situations through their identities and how mismatches between identity standards and the meaning of situations can lead to emotion and acting out. We also considered how different identities compete and how this may serve to curtail behavior. Identity theory in and as of itself does not offer a full explanation for HBV in that it is not clear precisely what honor or HBV identities would contain or how perceived consensus impacts upon behavior. We noted how shame is the likely emotion resulting from transgressions of honor and how this can lead to violent rage. However, we also noted that shame itself is not the only emotion relevant to HBV and fear of shame also may be an important emotion. We then considered the impact of the situation and how most of these theories had given little consideration to its importance.

All the models discussed had merit, but we argued that a full explanation for HBV requires a multilevel theory that considers the social, psychological, and situational context. In generating such a model, we applied the Theory of

Planned Behavior (TPB) to HBV and saw how this model provides a structure that allows consideration of HBV from multiple levels and explains it in terms of an interaction between social, psychological, and situational factors.

The model for HBV we have provided has a number of useful features. It provides an explanation that accounts for the data, and, importantly, suggests those conditions that increase or reduce the likelihood of HBV. This is particularly important when considering risk assessment and in designing prevention strategies as theory-driven approaches are likely to be more fruitful than ad hoc approaches. In the following chapter, this book will explore issues such as investigation, risk assessment, and prevention, and readers are invited to revisit this chapter to aid their understanding of these approaches.

In the next chapter, we move on to discuss the investigation of HBV allegations by law enforcement. We begin by exploring the role of the primary investigator.

Effective Investigation of Honor-Based Violence 1

3

Primary Investigation

In the following four chapters, we present proposals for the effective investigation of honor-based violence (HBV). For ease and clarity of presentation, we have divided the investigative process into two distinct phases: *primary* and *secondary* investigation. For each of these phases, we will describe the tasks and responsibilities of investigators that are required in order to maximize the likelihood of a successful outcome to the investigation.

The *primary investigation* phase is encapsulated by actions performed by frontline staff during the initial stages of an investigation, normally immediately following a report of suspected HBV. The *secondary investigation* phase is encapsulated by actions performed by specialist investigative staff, generally detectives, as part of the longer term investigation of a suspected HBV crime. This chapter deals with primary investigation and the following three chapters deal with secondary investigations.

It is important to note at the outset that HBV-related offenses provide the investigator with many complexities and challenges. As we have seen in Chapter 1, these offenses can be varied and the motivations of offenders can be difficult to understand. There is often significant press and community interest in HBV offending and the law enforcement response to it. Adding to the complexity, there are those in the community who would attempt to make political capital by stigmatizing particular communities as "supporters of HBV." As a result of all of this, the manner in which HBV crimes are investigated can have a significant impact upon the attitudes of the community toward, and their confidence in, law enforcement. It, therefore, is vital that these investigations are carried out with the upmost professionalism, integrity, and efficiency. Ultimately, however, it is the very complexity of HBV crimes that can defeat the investigators if they do not have access to adequate support and informed guidance when necessary. Our proposals are designed to demystify the investigation of HBV.

Law Enforcement Responsibilities

Most law enforcement personnel will be familiar with the *building block* principles of an investigation. These cover the most important responsibilities of law enforcement officers in response to any reported crime. These principles include:

- Preservation of life
- Preservation of crime scenes
- Securing evidence
- Identifying victims
- Identifying suspects (It is worth noting that there is often more than one suspect as HBV crimes frequently involve collusion and conspiracy.)

These building block principles should guide the response and actions of law enforcement officers throughout an investigation and, as readers will discover, these underpin our suggestions here.

First Report of an HBV Crime

Like other crimes, HBV-related crime can come to the attention of law enforcement in many ways, for example:

- A victim or their representative may make an allegation to front office staff at a law enforcement office.
- Law enforcement officers may be approached in the street with a report.
- A victim or his/her representative may telephone law enforcement either via a local number or an emergency number.
- Law enforcement officers may be called to an incident that has elements of HBV (see discussion of the characteristics of HBV in Chapter 2), such as a:
  - Domestic violence situation
  - Child abuse
  - Theft allegation
  - Missing person allegation
  - Dispute in the street
  - Other crimes in action, e.g., kidnap, false imprisonment, assault
  - Suicide attempt
  - Suicide
- Law enforcement may receive reports from other statutory agencies, e.g., social services, education, healthcare professionals, or other government agency.
- Law enforcement may receive a report directly from nongovernment organizations (NGOs).

Because of this variety there is a need for *all staff*, both law enforcement officers and civilian support workers, to have some awareness of HBV. Where there is a lack of knowledge, there is a risk that first reports of HBV will not be recognized and/or important investigative opportunities may be missed. Indeed. it is often the first response to a report that can dictate the success of any future investigation and management of risk (Association of Chief Police Officers, 2005).

Responding to a First Report

The response to a first report of HBV will depend upon the scenario. As detailed above, the need to preserve life is a fundamental requirement of law enforcement officers and, thus, ensuring the safety of individuals is paramount. Therefore, there are two questions that those receiving a first report need to consider immediately:

- How safe is the victim and anyone connected with the victim?
- What needs to be done immediately to ensure safety?

Clearly, where there is a crime in progress, there will be a need to affect an immediate emergency response that will involve law enforcement attendance at the scene.

It also is important to note that the characteristics of HBV impose an increased sense of urgency to act even when a crime is not in progress. We have noted that, in cases of HBV, victims face high risks of violence. The very fact that victims or someone connected with them have approached law enforcement either directly or indirectly can significantly increase the risk of violence they face; the act of reporting can be seen as "dishonoring" a family that is worthy of punishment. This means that, for all reports where HBV is suspected, it is advisable for an *immediate risk assessment* of the victim's situation to be carried out, followed by a plan of action that depends upon the identified risk level. Where risk is assessed as *high,* immediate steps should be taken to protect the victim. Risk management is discussed elsewhere in this book, so we do not intend to detail this process here; suffice it to say that once the victim's safety is ensured, the best possible primary investigation can commence.

Attitudes and Behavior Toward Those Reporting HBV

Reporting HBV to the police is often an individual's last resort. Law enforcement may be the only agency approached after months or even years of abuse. Victims and their representatives frequently express concerns around whether they will be believed, if they can trust law enforcement, and to what extent law enforcement supports perpetrators of HBV. These concerns are frequently related to their experiences in other jurisdictions where law enforcement corruption may be high and/or there is tacit institutional support for HBV perpetrators. It is vitally important, therefore, that anyone who receives a first report from victims or their representatives is able to engage with them in a professional, courteous, and supportive manner. It is important to take the allegations seriously, to listen carefully to the allegations, and to take steps to reassure that law enforcement does not support HBV perpetrators. Failure to do this is likely to result in the victims returning home to face continued abuse and/or an escalation of violence against them.

Recording of HBV

Any allegation of HBV should be recorded as a crime or crime-related incident so that the investigative process can be fully detailed, risks managed, and a rationale provided to decisions and strategies. Ideally, all HBV incidents should be flagged for monitoring purposes and to ensure the most appropriate investigative unit investigates these crimes. All actions, allegations, and details of individuals should be fully recorded and accuracy ensured. If possible, access to the recorded allegations should be limited because community members supportive of HBV may attempt to access the data to note the progress of the investigation, warn people of imminent arrests, or identify places of safety for the victim. If the data cannot be protected, then consideration needs to be given as to how investigative information will be recorded and stored.

Location of the Victim

Following a report of HBV, the location of the victim is an important consideration in determining all initial investigative decisions. There are two broad scenarios that may occur: these are where the victim's location is *presently unknown* and where the victim's location is *known* to law enforcement. Each of these scenarios demands different responses from primary investigators and these are considered below.

Victim's Location Is Unknown

If an allegation of HBV is made where the victim's location is presently unknown, then the individual taking the report should record the allegation on the relevant crime reporting databases and we suggest that it should be "flagged" as an HBV allegation. This is so the most suitable law enforcement unit or officers can be assigned to investigate the allegation. This also ensures that the allegation is adequately recorded for crime management purposes.

In addition to recording the allegation, a supervising officer and/or an on duty senior detective should be informed. This is because HBV presents a serious risk of violence and, thus, there is an urgent need for management decisions concerning how to proceed. If there is a specialist unit within an organization with responsibility for or expertise in the investigation of HBV crimes, steps should be taken, as a matter of urgency, to inform this group of the allegation so that it can initiate any secondary investigation deemed necessary.

Where law enforcement does not know the location of the victim, then sufficient enquiries need to be made to establish her whereabouts. This may include asking friends, workplace colleagues, school friends, or partners. However, great care should be taken if considering an approach to the family. It may well be that the family is the cause of the disappearance and may deliberately misinform law enforcement to cover their tracks or prevent the victim from being found. If an approach is to be made to a family member, then this should be done by an officer who has a sound understanding of HBV and who has a clear rationale as to why he/she is approaching that family member.

Where families themselves have approached law enforcement stating that the victim has run away from home or accusing the victim of a crime, it is often done to get law enforcement to act as de facto agents of the family to track down and bring the victim back to the family (see also the false allegations section below). Should law enforcement locate and return an individual to the family, this is often when the victim may be in gravest danger and subjected to the most serious crimes and violence as the family seeks to restore their "honor." And, the involvement of law enforcement in locating the victim may serve to compound family feelings of dishonor.

If an incident is brought to the attention of law enforcement by a third party, it is important that the identity of the third party is established, her details are verified, correct contact details are obtained, and attempts are made to establish if she knows where the victim is and whether she is safe. If possible, a senior detective, preferably one with an understanding of HBV, should speak to the third party at the time of the initial allegation.

If victims can be located, the ideal situation is to bring them to a law enforcement station or other location where their safety can be assured. This allows secondary investigating officers to manage the risk from a controlled environment. A victim should always be spoken to on her own in a room away from the sight and sound of others. Cultural considerations may mean that victims are uncomfortable speaking to male officers (although this may not always be the case) and, thus. it may be important to have a female officer speak to the victim.

Before a victim leaves the company of law enforcement officers, the relevant officers need to be satisfied that the victim's safety is assured. If the victim is a child and judged to be in imminent danger, then child protection measures should be invoked. If the victim is an adult and is unwilling to stay with law enforcement or go to some other place of safety, then the officer must document this, what has been done to ensure that person's safety, and what advice has been given. In most jurisdictions, it is important to note that law enforcement has no power to forcibly hold an adult victim of crime regardless of the danger she may face. While a victim of HBV is with law enforcement and prior to her leaving, consideration should be given to obtaining a photograph, fingerprints, and a DNA. Obtaining such information, however, should only be done with the victim's consent.

Victim's Location Is Known

Where the victim's location is presently known, there are a number of issues that need to be considered and actions that should be taken by primary investigators before a secondary investigation can begin. These will be considered and discussed below.

Immediate Response

In what follows, we will discuss the recommended actions of primary investigators following an allegation of HBV where the victim's location is presently known. The actions discussed follow directly from the above building blocks of investigations. We will discuss each action in the order that the primary investigator should carry them out.

Provision of or Request for Medical Aid   HBV victims can be in the presence of law enforcement officers for many reasons, such as following extreme violence, self-inflicted injuries, or sexual assault. Because of the need to preserve life, an injured victim's medical care is paramount; therefore, it is incumbent on initial investigating officers to provide, where required, emergency medical aid to victims or to seek assistance from medical professionals. However, any attending law enforcement officer should be mindful of the need to obtain and secure evidence that may support a future prosecution. This is best done by effective communication with medical professionals either at the scene or in a medical environment. It is important to note that while medical personnel are trained in saving lives, they are unlikely to be trained in evidential retrieval and the potential evidential importance of items taken from the victim. As such, primary investigators need to ensure, where possible, that the evidential value of any items that are removed from the victim are preserved as much as is possible.

Often victims of HBV suffer such significant injuries that nonmedical personnel believe that the victim is either dead or about to die. Even in situations such as this, it is recommended that medical aid should be sought or provided until a medical practitioner has declared the person deceased.

Scenes of Crimes

In this section, we provide advice for the primary investigator when attending crime scenes that may involve HBV.

Multiple Crime Scenes

Initial investigating officers should be aware that, as with any offense, there may be a number of relevant crime scenes where evidence could be obtained. As such, they need to consider not only the scene where the victim was found, but also consider the existence of other possible scenes, including:

- Location where the victim was last seen alive
- Initial contact site between victim and offender
- Attack site
- Deposition site
- Potential travel routes of the victim
- Potential travel routes of the offender and accomplices
- Vehicles used by victim and/or suspect

Initial Crime Scene Response

When the initial investigating officer has identified an HBV crime scene, there are a number of steps that should be taken to avoid unnecessary disturbance to the scene by law enforcement, witnesses, or others.

Crime Scene Preservation

It is likely the initial investigating officer will be the first law enforcement person at the crime scene and, as with other offenses, they should note the exact details of the scene, such as where the victim is, signs of disturbance, any blood or weapons, etc. If at all possible, the initial investigating officer should try to capture this information on a digital camera, though this should not replace the photos taken by a professionally trained forensic photographer. If it is not possible to take digital pictures, then sketches could suffice detailing the whereabouts of significant items.

One of the major responsibilities of the initial attending officer is the preservation of evidence at the scene. They should prevent to the best of their ability:

- Movement of exhibits
- Evidence being obliterated
- Additional material being added
- Loss of evidence
- Disturbance at the scene
- Destruction of the scene and evidence

Following are some useful steps that initial investigating officers can take in order to protect the crime scene as much as possible:

- Consideration should be given to the entry and exit points for all personnel that minimizes disturbance to the scene, although it should be noted that this point may be the same entry/exit point of any suspect(s).
- Gloves and disposable shoe covers should be worn, if the circumstances allow, when entering the scene.
- Surfaces or objects should not be touched.
- If material has to be touched or moved, this should be recorded in terms of what it is and why it had to be touched or moved.
- If nonlaw enforcement personnel are in attendance, i.e., other emergency services, primary investigators should try and note what they have touched, moved, and where they have been. If at all possible, they should wear gloves and disposable shoe covers to assist in protecting the integrity of the scene.
- Details should be obtained for all people in attendance at the scene so that the investigating officer can obtain statements from them detailing what they have done at the scene, what they touched, and where they have been. It may be necessary to obtain these people's fingerprints, DNA, boot prints, etc., for elimination purposes.
- When opening doors and windows, investigators should do so from points that would normally not be used, e.g., top or bottom.
- Investigating officers should try and use a different (less obvious) route in and out of the crime scene than the suspect may have used, being mindful of where they are treading and what is on the walls. In HBV, it is generally the case that the victim and suspect are known to each other and the suspect may have legitimate access to the premises; therefore, marks on walls, e.g., bloody fingerprints, blood splatters, will be significant.

If the victim has to be taken from the scene, then this should be done with the minimum of disturbance to the scene. This may prove difficult depending upon the victim's injuries and the medical personnel or other emergency services that have been present. As previously stated, the injuries suffered by HBV victims can be serious, including multiple stab injuries, burning, or acid attacks, and this may require significant medical or safety intervention.

Regardless of the complications in the initial scene management, the initial investigating officers need, as far as possible, to take control of the scene and manage entry into that scene. Entry should be restricted to only those who need to enter, i.e., medical personal, fire and rescue personnel, investigating officers, and crime scene examiners.

The initial investigating officer should start a *scene and incident management log* to record all actions at the scene, including what has been done at the scene, what has been moved or taken away from the scene, and the reasons for doing so, as well as recording who has entered the scene and when and why. This information may be crucial, particularly if forensic evidence becomes critical for the case progression.

HBV victims may be aware that they are about to be attacked and may take steps to escape, which could result in multiple attack sites in many rooms. There also may be more than one victim or offender. As such, on initial attendance at the crime scene, a flash search should be completed to identify additional attack scenes or locate other victims or offenders.

A crime scene examiner should be called at the earliest opportunity to assist in scene preservation, seizing, and packaging of exhibits, and to make an assessment of the scene itself to decide if further support is needed.

Cordoning off the Crime Scene

The primary investigator should cordon off the crime scene as appropriate in the circumstances. Following that, it may be necessary, dependent on the scene type, to request specialist support services to prevent loss or destruction of evidence. By the nature of many HBV crimes, the scene may be in an area or location inhabited or frequently visited by both the victim and perpetrator. However, this should not prevent the usual scene preservation measures being taken because significant evidential retrieval is still possible.

Inner and Outer Cordons

Ideally the most effective way to control a crime scene is to establish an *inner* and *outer* cordon. The inner cordon will include where the victim was found and all possible entry and exit routes used by a suspect or suspects. The outer cordon should be large enough to include a rendezvous point for law enforcement officers and a marshalling area for official vehicles. If uncertain, it is better to overestimate the cordon size as this then can be reduced following expert analysis. Within the inner cordon, anyone entering, as far as possible, should always wear protective clothing and use the designated entry and exit routes.

The cordons can be designated by the use of law enforcement tape. However, dependent on the scene, the type of incident, and its location, other specialized equipment may be required, such as tents and lighting protective barriers. The initial attending officers should be aware that there may be a need to protect the scene from prying eyes, such as the general public or media. HBV investigations can generate a large press interest and it may be worthwhile considering a press cordon area.

In respect to the cordons, any attending officers or other emergency personal should be mindful of revealing who they are at the outer cordon in case they are overheard, e.g., a murder squad detective announcing he or she is from the murder squad. This may unintentionally inform suspects, the community, or the press what the incident is. When officers are talking inside the cordon about the incident, they should be mindful of who can overhear them as comments overheard can be revealed by the press or be subject of local gossip.

Cordon Management

When a scene is secured, there is a need for it to be managed by a *cordon officer* who is responsible for managing who enters and leaves the crime scene. The cordon officer should start a *crime scene log* that records all parties who visit and/or go into the scene. The details he/she should record include the individual's name, status (e.g., family member, forensic officer, etc.), and the date and time of attendance. It is imperative that the information recorded in this document is passed to the secondary investigation team at the earliest opportunity. This information can be highly significant because, in the case of HBV, it is not unknown for the perpetrator and accomplices to attend the scene in order to gauge the progress of the law enforcement investigation and/or to interfere with evidence identification and retrieval.

The cordon officer should remain at his/her posting at all times to ensure continuity and prevent people from entering the cordon inadvertently or on purpose. The only time the cordon officer should move is when he/she is relieved by another cordon officer and this should be recorded in the cordon log as well.

Legal Powers to Enforce Cordons

Dependent on legal jurisdiction will be the powers law enforcement can use to control cordons and prevent access to land and premises. In the United Kingdom, there are no statutory powers to cordon off land or buildings and prevent access. Law enforcement is reliant on common law powers.

To accommodate the needs of common law, it is important that the officer in charge should record the following:

- The gravity of the offense for which the area is cordoned off
- The precise area cordoned off
- Why it is considered reasonable to cordon this particular area off

- The necessity in cordoning the area off
- Considerations with respect to local jurisdiction
- Victim, family, and community considerations

Cordons should not be released until the officer in charge of the investigation authorizes their release.

Access to Crime Scenes

Rights of access to crime scenes will be dictated by local statute. There may be specific powers laid down in statute, e.g., the U.K. Section 17 of the Law Enforcement and Criminal Evidence Act allows entry by force to protect life and limb. However, consideration may be needed to obtain a court warrant or legal authority to secure access to premises or private land. The need to obtain a court warrant should not be prohibitive to setting up a cordon around premises.

Where a crime scene has been subject to a law enforcement cordon, if a private person wishes access, the reason for and the legitimacy of that request needs to be carefully considered. If a person has a right of access, such as being a resident at the scene, where this can be achieved without disrupting the crime scene, it is often best that such a request should be allowed in the interests of law enforcement community relations. If, however, there is any likelihood that the request would seriously disrupt the crime scene, leading to the loss or adding of material, then the request should be politely refused and this should be explained to the person. This decision should be made by a supervisor and preferably by the senior investigating officer or his/her representative. If the person still insists on going in to the cordoned-off area, then law enforcement should consider what powers they have to prevent the person entering the area, e.g., under U.K. law, offenses exist, such as obstructing law enforcement or attempting to pervert the course of justice.

Wider Scene Considerations

A crime scene assessment should be carried out as soon as possible by a suitably qualified crime scene examiner, preferably with some knowledge of HBV crimes. This is so that an effective and appropriate crime scene management strategy can be initiated. This initial strategy should include photography, identification of fast track forensic submissions, common approach paths to and from the scene, and the appropriate size of cordons. The initial investigating officer should be mindful as well of entry and egress points to enable the identification of potential witnesses and of closed circuit TV (CCTV) points. It is worthwhile noting also that it is not only the customary forensic issues that have to be considered, but also telephones, computers, computer tablets, other digital hardware, diaries, and other written documentation.

Forensic Considerations

When a crime scene has been properly secured and cordoned, forensic examination can commence. There are a number of forensic considerations that apply to HBV and these are discussed below.

Packaging of Exhibits

If items have to be removed from the scene prior to the arrival of specialist exhibits officers, it is paramount that they are packaged correctly. Advice should be sought from a crime scene examiner or specialist trained exhibits officer.

Victim Examination

Dependent on the allegation and how recent the incident was, the victim should be considered as a crime scene. The clothes she was wearing at the time of the offense should be identified and seized, regardless of whether they have been removed or washed. There still may be the opportunity to obtain relevant forensic evidence from such items.

Consideration also should be given to photographing the victim and her injuries as well as having them examined by a forensic medical practitioner, who will be able to evidence the injuries and may be able to give an opinion as to how those injuries were caused. If the victim has been subjected to a sexual assault, then a specialist-trained sexual investigations officer should be called at the earliest opportunity to maximize the potential of obtaining forensic evidence and to ensure that the victim is afforded the most appropriate support.

Victims

There are a number of considerations for primary investigators pertaining to the treatment of victims that are important in HBV cases and we consider these below. It is especially important for primary investigators to be mindful that, in cases of HBV, the victims may have inflicted serious injury or even death on themselves.

Victim Taken to the Hospital

If a victim is taken to hospital, primary investigators should record the names of the paramedics and details of the vehicle they have used. The ambulance that the victim travelled in can be considered a crime scene and, thus, it may be necessary to seize it. Advice should be sought from a senior supervisor who will liaise with senior paramedics regarding the removal of the ambulance from duty should this be necessary.

If possible, a law enforcement officer should travel to the hospital with the victim to provide evidence or continuity, coordinate investigations at the hospital, and offer protection to the victim. The initial investigating officers should be aware that the injuries to the victim may be the result of a failed attempted murder and the family may consider coming to the hospital to complete their task. Officers should not underestimate the extent families or their associates will go to finish the job and restore family honor. If it is not possible to send an officer from the scene, then an officer should be at the hospital at the earliest opportunity.

It is important to reiterate that the victim is a crime scene in her own right and, therefore, at the hospital, all clothing and possessions should be seized and packaged. If the initial investigating officer is not trained in crime exhibits, then he/she should be supported by an exhibits trained officer or take advice from such an officer or crime scene investigator. This is to ensure continuity and forensically protect the integrity of the exhibits. At the hospital, law enforcement officers should request pretransfusion blood and inform the investigating officer that this has been taken. Hospitals will only keep pretransfusion blood for a limited time and will often require a written request or court order to release the blood.

There is a high potential of losing a significant amount of forensic evidence at the hospital and, as already stated, preservation of life must come first. Attending officers should not hinder the work of the medical professionals, but every opportunity to obtain as much evidence as possible should be taken without interfering with the hospital staffs' work. This will involve good communication channels between medical practitioners and attending officers. The attending officers should obtain the details of all medical personnel working on the victim, so that statements can be obtained from them at a later date.

Once medical practitioners finish their work and, in agreement with them, the officer should consider speaking to the victim if she is conscious in order to obtain as many details as possible about the incident. Any information provided should be recorded because this may be of significance.

It is important that the officer tries to obtain family details from relevant witnesses including the victim while at the hospital. In particular, details of other family members, who the head of the family is, details of family members potentially at risk, details of previous attacks (if any), and the motivation behind this attack are all important when investigating HBV. The officer should obtain a medical prognosis as well about the victim's condition in order to make informed decisions in respect to how the investigation will be managed.

Victim Statements

Due to the complexity of honor crimes, it is advised that only specially trained officers with knowledge of HBV should take initial statements from victims. Only in exceptional circumstances should an initial investigating officer without thorough knowledge of HBV consider taking such a statement. Prior to taking the statement, the initial investigating officer should inform his/her supervisor and the most senior detective on duty of the circumstances and take advice from them. If an initial investigating officer has to take a statement, he/she must record why the statement had to be taken at that time and why it could not have waited for a specialist trained officer or detective to take the statement

Victim Has Died

Where the victim has died, the role of the initial investigating officer is to protect and secure the crime scene, identify if there are any further victims or likely victims, and await support from homicide specialists.

If the initial investigating officer attends the scene or is at the hospital and the victim is seriously injured, he/she should make every effort to establish who was responsible for the injuries and, where possible, record the exact words spoken by the victim or any indications she makes. Even if the injuries are self-inflicted, it is important to attempt to establish why the person has inflicted these injuries and if other family members are victims or at risk of HBV. This information may be admissible as evidence in court as a dying declaration.

Informing Next of Kin

The task of informing next of kin should always be done with tact and diplomacy, but, when the incident is believed an HBV incident, this task should be carried out by an experienced officer and one who has knowledge of HBV. If at all possible, a family liaison officer (FLO) or similar skilled officer should be considered for this role. Because the family may be the perpetrators of the crime, careful consideration needs to be given to how this is done and when it is done.

The initial investigating officer should record who the details were given to and their reactions. The officer also should record if there were any individuals that he/she was not allowed to see when informing next of kin, notably female members of the family.

Because of the international nature of HBV, the family may not be local to that law enforcement area, region, or country. Then, liaison will be needed with other law enforcement agencies, consulates, and governments. It is not possible to detail precisely the processes involved as these will vary depending on the jurisdictions involved.

Witnesses

In this section, we will consider issues related to witnesses of HBV, because they pertain to initial investigating officers.

Locating Witnesses

Identifying potential witnesses and getting them to speak to law enforcement or any other agency can be a challenge for anyone investigating HBV. Family members or other victims often are unwilling to speak out for fear of dishonoring their family and community, or for fear of the consequences of speaking out. If witnesses are present and willing to talk to law enforcement, the primary investigator should obtain and verify their details. Similarly, if the initial investigating officer is able to identify further potential witnesses by other investigative means, then these details also should be taken and recorded for future contact. It is worth noting that the contact details of potential witnesses should always be taken even if the initial investigating officer believes that they will not talk to law enforcement.

Taking Witness Statements

It is preferable that witness statements always should be taken by a secondary investigating officer who is either a detective or who has knowledge of HBV—preferably both. Only in exceptional circumstances should an initial investigating officer take a witness statement. Prior to taking *any* witness statement, primary investigators should obtain approval from a supervisor or senior duty detective.

Should an initial investigating officer have to take a witness statement, then he/she needs to consider the status of the witness very carefully. If the witness is a child or a significant witness, then the initial investigating officer should *only* proceed if he/she has specialist training in interviewing children and/or significant witnesses. A *significant witness* is an individual who has *seen* or *heard* an offense or someone *deemed* as significant by a senior investigating officer. If the witness is judged to be peripheral to the investigation, e.g., his/her information is judged not to be critical, the initial investigating officer may take the statement. Again, a rational explanation of the reason for taking the statement needs to be recorded. The reason is that, in the early stages of an investigation as complex as an HBV, someone who at first appears on the periphery could, in fact, be a key witness or even a suspect.

Suspects

In this section, we consider issues related to suspects of concern to the initial investigating officer.

Identification of Suspects

The early identification and arrest of suspects is a priority for any law enforcement officer. However, in HBV investigations, this is often complicated as there may be more than one suspect, collusion, or conspiracy. Initial investigating officers should try and concentrate their efforts on identifying and locating primary suspects, though, if additional suspects, such as other conspirators, are identified, they should be arrested as well.

When a suspect or suspects are identified, initial investigating officers should record how the suspect has been identified and by whom, who they believe to be the primary suspect, and who else they believe to be involved. There are also a number of important additional considerations that we will detail below.

Intelligence

Where a suspect is identified, the initial investigating officer should consider what is known about the suspect, i.e., the level of violence he used; the weapons used; any premises he owns, occupies, or controls; the suspect's access to vehicles; the suspect's criminal history and previous law enforcement contact, most notably around family or childcare/safety issues. By making an immediate assessment of all these factors, an officer can make a more informed assessment of the risk that the suspect or suspects may pose to other family members or the wider community.

Arrest

In the event that an arrest is possible, a decision has to be made in respect to the timing of the arrest. This has to be balanced against loss of evidence, safety of others, and the requirements of the investigation. Our advice is to arrest at the earliest opportunity when all other safety issues are taken into account, unless there are significant reasons for not doing so. Once a suspect is in custody, investigating officers can manage the issues of detention and evidential recovery. It is important that if a decision to arrest is made, the reasons for it should be recorded in as much detail as possible. The detention of anyone who is arrested should be handled by specialist trained custody officers and in line with the policies and practices of the relevant jurisdiction.

When the initial investigating officers make arrests, they should be mindful of cross-contamination issues. If at all possible, the arresting officer should not be an officer who has been to the crime scene or had contact with the victim or a significant witness. If there has been contact of this type, before the officer can make the arrest, he/she should fully document what contact he/she has had with the crime scene, victim, or witnesses.

It is very important that anything that a suspect says prior to and after his arrest is recorded at the earliest opportunity. Frequently, these comments may have some investigative and even evidential value.

Following the arrest, the suspect or suspects should not be taken to the same law enforcement office as victims or witnesses to avoid any future allegation of cross contamination or potential intimidation. If there is more than one suspect, consideration should be given to taking them to different offices.

In cases of HBV, sometimes individuals do hand themselves into custody. In such cases, the individuals concerned should be arrested and subject to a suspect interview. Officers should be particularly mindful of individuals giving themselves into custody who are youths or under the age of criminal responsibility. It is not unusual in HBV cases for families to offer up younger members of the family as the perpetrators in the expectation that they may get a lesser sentence than an adult.

Verification of Details

It is important that, once arrested, the details of the person in custody are verified and confirmed. This can be done by means of viewing legal documentation, e.g., passports, driving licenses, or via fingerprints. If the person is believed to be a foreign national or has dual citizenship, then overseas checks must be carried out. This is especially important in HBV investigations because of the international nature of honor crimes. All suspects' details should be recorded fully and accurately on a crime-recording database.

Suspect Examination

If a suspect has been arrested, consideration should be given to whether he or she is a crime scene and the opportunity of obtaining forensic evidence from them. The following is a list of some of the potential forensic opportunities that may be obtained from a suspect:

- Suspect injuries: Primary investigators are advised to obtain photographs of any injuries or marks the suspect may have regardless of how the suspect says he/she obtained those injuries.

- Suspect fingerprints: This may include an electronic copy and a "wet" set.
- Suspect nail clippings.
- Swabs from the suspect's skin.
- DNA swabs.
- Investigators are advised to seize a suspect's clothing.
- Investigators should obtain footwear impressions of the suspect's footwear.
- Suspect's hair samples should be obtained, including pubic hair, if appropriate.
- Investigators should seize electronic and digital hardware owned by the suspect, i.e., phones, laptops, etc.

It is important to note, however, that, depending on the local legislation, some of these samples may only be taken with the appropriate authority obtained from either a senior law enforcement officer or a court of law. The obtaining of samples may vary depending on the offense type, its circumstances, the age of the crime, and the relationship between victim and suspect, and, thus, the above should not be seen as an exhaustive list. Where HBV is suspected, it is important, even for seemingly lesser crimes, that full consideration is given to maximizing evidential retrieval from a suspect.

Supervision of Primary Investigations

Due to the nature, complexity, and risk associated with HBV investigations, if the initial investigating officers believe or someone informs them that honor may be an issue, they *must* request a supervisor attend the crime scene or meet with the officer at the earliest opportunity. Upon arrival, the supervisor should assume responsibility for managing how the primary investigation will be progressed including liaising with detectives who will provide investigative expertise.

If for any reason there is a delay in a supervisory officer attending, then best practice is to record the delay and the reasons for it. This is also true if the supervising officer cannot attend and delegates supervisory control to another. These two points are especially important where a scene has to be managed, there is a real and credible threat to life, of immediate violence, or of any other honor issue, e.g., forced marriage, female genital mutilation.

Until a supervisory officer arrives, the first officer or most senior officer in attendance will assume responsibility. Again, best practice indicates that who this officer is should be recorded and, when responsibility is handed to another person, that should be recorded as well.

When the allegation is recorded on a crime database, this should be supervised at the earliest opportunity to ensure that minimum investigative standards have been met, the risk to the victim or any other person is being effectively managed, the relevant people who need to be informed have been informed (i.e., investigating officers, senior management), and any short falls in the primary investigation can be rectified at the earliest opportunity. The responsibility for ensuring that frontline supervisors have completed their role should be with a senior supervisor. In the United Kingdom, that would be an officer of inspector rank, also known as the duty officer.

Role of the Senior Supervisor (Duty Officer)

The duty officer should be informed at once of any allegation or investigation where it is believed honor may be an issue; that basically means any crime allegation, missing person enquiry, fear of crime about to take place, threats to victims (such as threat of forced carriage), or allegations from outside of his/her jurisdiction.

The duty officer should be responsible for all serious, violent, high-risk incidents involving HBV. He/she will manage and supervise all officers and staff pending a formal handing over to a detective or other secondary investigative officers.

It is good practice for duty officers to undertake the following;

- Be responsible for all crime scenes, keeping them open and appropriately staffed until they are released by the senior investigating officer.
- Conducting a formal face-to-face briefing with a detective or other secondary investigating officer to hand the investigation over in a controlled and managed way.
- Brief his/her senior manager on the incident itself, what investigation has taken place, risks to the organization, and resource issues. Resourcing HBV allegations can involve a high level of investment in staff, equipment, and time; therefore, if additional resources are needed, it should be a duty officer who requests these resources, recording what resources are needed, why, and for how long he/she anticipates that they are needed.

Conclusion

In this chapter, we have considered some of the important issues in the primary investigation of HBV. We have seen that HBV crimes are likely to present the investigator with significant challenges and it is this complexity that may undermine a successful investigation. We have noted, however, that a systematic approach to primary investigation, utilization of generic investigative skills, and a clear understanding of investigative priorities and responsibilities are likely to minimize the risks to an investigation. In the next chapter, we move on to consider the secondary investigation of HBV.

Effective Investigation of Honor-Based Violence 2

4

Secondary Investigation

In the previous chapter, we explored the primary investigation of honor-based violence (HBV) crimes. In this chapter, we move on to consider secondary investigation. To recap, we define *secondary investigation* as those actions performed by specialist investigative officers, generally detectives, as part of the longer-term investigation of a suspected HBV crime.

A secondary investigation begins when a detective or specialist investigator takes over the investigative responsibility from a primary investigator. At the point this happens will vary with respect to the specific circumstances of a given offense and there is likely to be some overlap in the tasks carried out by primary and secondary investigators. It may be that, in some jurisdictions, investigators may take on many of the tasks described in this and the previous chapter.

In the following section, we focus specifically on tasks that are generally considered to fall within the realm of detective work. Typically, these tasks begin after a primary investigation has established that a crime has been committed and, where relevant, has identified some or all of the crime scenes and secured them. With any crime there is a need to establish what happened, to whom, how, and why, and evidence needs to be collected that will allow the identification, arrest, and prosecution of suspects. Secondary investigation, therefore, incorporates tasks that support these needs and includes developing forensic and other investigative strategies; identifying and obtaining accounts from victims and witnesses; and the identification, interviewing, arrest, and charging of suspects.

Specialist Investigators

As we have pointed out, the investigation of HBV-related offenses has the potential to be an extremely complex and lengthy process that can involve allegations of serious and multiple criminalities. As a result, we recommend that *specially trained* investigators take on the secondary investigator role in investigating HBV. By specially trained, we suggest detective officers experienced in general crime investigation with specialist training in HBV.

Crime Scene Considerations

Following the work of the primary investigator, the secondary investigator has a number of responsibilities with respect to a crime scene where one is identified. These complement and serve as a quality assurance check on the work of primary investigators. As such, we strongly recommend that secondary investigators should make a point of visiting crime scenes. There are a number of important benefits of this that we consider below.

Crime Scene Management

The adequate preservation and management of any crime scene is of paramount importance to any investigator. This is particularly so with HBV crimes where, due to the (often) close proximity and/or relationships between victim and suspect, the smallest detail and the context in which evidence may be found can have a huge bearing on the outcome on any investigation. By visiting the crime scene, secondary investigators can establish if there are adequate controls of the scene in place. For example, are cordons appropriately placed and is entry to the scene being managed appropriately? If it is necessary to change cordons, the investigator should record to where cordons were moved and why they were moved.

Crime Scene Assessment

In visiting a crime scene while it is under law enforcement control, secondary investigators will be able to view it noting the relationship of its characteristics before evidence is lost. This is important in developing a crime scene assessment. A crime scene assessment is an important step for secondary investigators because this will enable them to begin to develop investigative strategies. Following a crime scene assessment, the investigator should be in a position to better direct and focus resources, and generate and test hypotheses.

In order to carry out a comprehensive crime scene assessment, it is important that investigators have clear aims and objectives of what they want to achieve. These objectives may be in consultation with primary investigating officers, crime scene investigators, and their own knowledge of HBV crimes.

In addition to general considerations that pertain to any crime scene assessment, such as nature and location of forensic evidence, in cases of HBV, we advise that particular attention is paid to

- Material that was taken to or from the scene by the suspect or victim. In HBV this is particularly pertinent if the items do not fit in with cultural beliefs, e.g. alcohol or items for restraint

- Identification of access and egress routes from the scene—this may be pertinent where victims have been removed from an initial attack site in the home to a deposition site or holding location (if the victim had been kidnapped and held against her will)
- Identification of CCTV or other passive data generators that may provide useful information/evidence for the enquiry.

Cross Contamination

The secondary investigator should consider cross contamination of forensic exhibits particularly where initial investigating officers may have had contact with the victim, witnesses, and suspects. It is essential that processes and procedures are put in place to ensure cross contamination does not occur or, if it does, it is minimized. This is particularly an issue in HBV where suspect and witnesses may live in the same home and where the home is the crime scene.

Crime Scene Search

Once a scene has been forensically examined, the investigator should consider (if this has not already been completed) undertaking a comprehensive search of the crime scene and surrounding area. To facilitate, an investigator may consider the use of specialist trained search officers. Clear objectives should be set by the lead investigator for the search. This is where previous knowledge and expertise of HBV incidents is necessary so that search teams can be briefed on what items to look for, e.g., victim's diaries, paperwork, communication devices, computers, because victims have been known to record their ongoing abuse in many formats, and/or perpetrators may contact other conspirators to plan an offense.

Appointment of a Crime Scene Investigator

Where an offense is particularly serious, the lead investigator should consider working with a *crime scene investigator (CSI)* who will play an active role in managing all aspects of scene examination. The advantage of this is that many of the issues discussed above can be managed by this specialist including issues of cross contamination, the management of large numbers of exhibits, and advising on the requirement of specialist services. In addition, on the advice of a CSI, it may be appropriate to obtain the services of other specialist advisors, such as biologists, archeologists, entomologists, etc.

Ideally, if a specific CSI is appointed, he should have some knowledge of HBV investigations and, if not, then the investigating officer should fully brief him on the complexities he may face with this type of investigation, e.g., the risk of families destroying, removing, or altering evidence to support the suspect and/or frustrate the investigation.

Where a CSI is engaged in an investigation, it is important that an effective and regular communication channel is set between the investigator and the CSI so that expectations and requirements are effectively managed.

Recording of Crime Scenes

HBV crime scenes can be particularly difficult to interpret especially where they have been corrupted to frustrate an investigation. Therefore, it is important that the crime scenes are accurately recorded. The reasons for this include:

- Reinforcing the integrity of evidence recovered from the scene
- Evidencing links between scenes
- Highlighting and making explicit the basis for any scene interpretation
- Facilitating any reinterpretation of scenes as new information comes to light
- Supporting investigating officers briefings
- Presentation of evidence at court

How this information is recorded will be dependent on the circumstances, such as the complexity of the scene, the sustainability of the scene (including its potential for deterioration and the time available for the scene to be retained by law enforcement), and the geographical location of the scene. Media that could be considered for recording scenes include: written records, scene plans, photographs, video, 360 degree photography, aerial photography, virtual reconstruction, surveying equipment, or computer applications, such as Google Earth.

Release of the Crime Scene

Once the investigating officer is satisfied that all evidential opportunities have been exploited and expert advice (if appropriate) has been taken into account, consideration should be given to releasing the scene. This can be a particularly difficult decision with HBV cases as the investigating officer may be releasing the scene back to individuals who may have had some involvement in the offense. It is recommended, therefore, that a scene only be released when investigators feel that all the evidential potential of the scene has been realized.

Forensic Considerations

The development of a clear and concise forensic strategy is a key priority for any HBV investigation as the investigating officer will often find himself subject to false and misleading information from family and community members in an attempt to derail any police investigation and to protect the suspects.

As with other investigations, forensic evidence can be used to:

- Clarify circumstances
- Trace, implicate, or eliminate individuals
- Garner intelligence
- Identify and prioritize lines of enquiry
- Support interview strategies
- Clarify sequence of events
- Prioritize submission of materials for examination in a lab
- Link scenes

The development of a forensic strategy should start when the investigator attends a crime scene. It should be recognized that the forensic strategy will develop in line as the enquiry matures and the case develops.

Key considerations in developing a forensic strategy should include:

- Obtaining physical material from either the victim and/or suspect, such as clothing, objects in their possession, body samples, and/or swabs.
- Victim incapacitation: This is particularly relevant to HBV as kidnap and false imprisonment are often key constituents of HBV crimes.
- Sexual evidence: HBV victims may be raped before the primary attack takes place.
- Forensic awareness: Families and community members may be supportive of HBV and may attempt to frustrate a police investigation, such as attempting to destroy evidence or mislead investigators by presenting an honor killing as a suicide.
- Offender injuries: HBV offenders will claim they are victims of crime themselves; hence, it is important that any injuries discovered on a suspect are properly recorded and examined by a medical expert who can provide an evidential opinion as to how the injuries have been caused. In inflicting injuries on the victim, offenders also may have injured themselves, and this will need to be properly documented and recorded. All injuries should be photographed by a professional or appropriately trained photographer.
- Missing items: Families practicing HBV will often remove personal items from an HBV victim in an attempt to frustrate victim identification.

- Blood distribution: Blood distribution evidence may provide significant information to allow a more objective interpretation of events. This can be significant in HBV cases where what family members tell police is not necessarily true.
- Linking evidence: Often there is more than one scene in HBV cases, e.g., an initial attack site, vehicles used to transport the victim away from the site, another location where the victim is incapacitated, and, if the victim is killed, a deposition site. If an investigating officer can link these sites to the victim and offenders, this greatly supports any future criminal justice case.

It is important that the lead investigator undertakes regular forensic reviews to ensure that the overall forensic strategy is being met, appropriate resources are deployed effectively, and to drive future decision making.

Where the case is particularly serious or complex, consideration should be given by the lead investigating officer of formulating a Forensic Management Team, which could include the following people: the lead investigating officer, his deputy, scientific manager, CSI, exhibits officer, forensic manager, forensic advisor. This list is by no means exhaustive. The objective of this team should be the management of scientific resources, provision of scene management, coordination and operational advice, and strategic management of scientific supports services to meet the needs of the investigation. This team can provide a forum of advice to a lead investigator ensuring he had comprehensive knowledge of the forensic case and has access to the right forensic support.

Pathology

Where the victim has been killed or a suicide is linked to HBV, the investigator will have to consider pathology evidence. This will include how the victim died (if possible, where and when), evidence of weapons used, and the removal of the body from the scene. In cases of HBV, the general health of the deceased prior to death is also very significant. In honor killings, the victim often has been physically or sexually assaulted prior to the murder, and, in suicides, some victims may have suffered genital mutilation or years of abuse. Some injuries that are identified may be old injuries, but relevant to the case in question and will be further evidence of the systematic abuse the victim may have suffered. In suicide cases, investigating officers should be particularly mindful of whether duress was a part of the death or whether any other surviving members are at risk of being the victims of serious criminality. There are a number of other considerations for the investigator related to pathology that we discuss below.

Attendance of the Pathologist at the Crime Scene

Dependent on when and where the body was found, the investigating officer needs to consider whether the attendance of the pathologist is required at the scene so that he can view the body in context and assist in scene interpretation, which may then help decide investigative strategies. We would advise that, if there is more than one body discovered, then a pathologist is called as a matter of course to the scene to undertake his initial examinations.

The type of pathology examination that will be required should be a matter of discussion between the lead investigator and the pathologist and will be influenced by the condition of the body, how the person may have died, and the age of the deceased. Consideration also should be given to radiological examination of the body and examination by other specialists, such as odontologist, biologists, toxicologists, entomologists, and anthropologists.

If a pathologist does attend the scene, then the lead investigator should fully brief him of his belief that this is an honor killing or related suicide, and the consequences of this for any investigative process. It is important that, if the pathologist has no awareness of HBV, part of the briefing should include a summary of the nature of honor crimes. This will then enable the pathologist to make informed decisions about how to conduct a postmortem. Any taking and removal of specimens by the pathologist at the scene should be done in consultation with the lead investigator.

Postmortem

Once the lead investigator is happy that all forensic considerations have been achieved at the scene, including any relevant photography (whether with a pathologist attending or not), then the body should be removed to a mortuary. Prior to the start of any postmortem, the pathologist should be given a full briefing with the case to date. The relationship between the pathologist and the lead investigator should be ongoing throughout the investigation because, as is the nature of honor killings, a significant amount of information and facts are not always known at the point of first postmortem. As witness evidence is obtained and forensic results become known, the pathologist's opinion of how, the cause of, and why a victim may have died can be determined.

Time of Death

When a body has been *in situ* for a length of time, an assessment of the time of death will be difficult; therefore, the investigating officer should consider how he is going to determine a time of death. Generally, factual evidence of when the victim was last seen is the most accurate determinate, far more so than the condition of the body and the environment in which it is placed. However, with honor killings, this may prove difficult as evidence presented by family members may be purposefully inaccurate as a means of frustrating a criminal enquiry. The lead investigating officer should make these facts known to the pathologist and consider using other methods to determine time of death, for example:

- Last known usage of victim's phone/other communication data not withstanding a victim's access to this equipment as it may indicate when they were incarcerated/incapacitated rather than murdered.
- Scientific techniques, e.g., use of an entomologist.
- Last contact with friends, colleagues, acquaintances.
- Appearance on passive data generators, e.g., CCTV, records of use of bank/credit cards (notwithstanding the potential for suspects to use the cards).
- Use of social media, such as Facebook, Twitter, etc.

Identification of Victims

A key feature of honor killings, particularly if the body has been *in situ* for some time, is identification, because some families may not be supportive of any identification process, particularly if they have been a participant in the cause of death.

Where law enforcement is unable to identify a victim, they may need to undertake antemortem harvest of information of the deceased, such as fingerprints, DNA, medical information, or odontology, and unique medical references (e.g., serial numbered hip replacement joint) with secondary features also being considered, such as body marks/scars, tattoos, and/or significant bodily features to confirm identify. This will mean identifying features (marks, tattoos, scars, or medical procedures) to be photographed. It is recommended that the use of the Interpol Disaster Victim Identification forms are considered, particularly if the body remains unidentified.

Determining Fatal Injuries

Where the victim has suffered multiple injuries, as is often the case in honor killings, the pathologist needs to determine what the fatal injury was. It obviously is critical in any homicide investigation that the lead investigator understands how the victim died and the pathologist's reasons for coming to this conclusion. It may be, as the enquiry matures, information will challenge the pathologist's opinion and a reassessment will be needed.

Attendance at Postmortem

We advise that the lead investigator or his deputy should attend the postmortem to assist the pathologist with interpretation issues. This is especially important with honor killings where there can be multiple, significant injuries often inflicted by more than one person as well as the likelihood of sexual assaults. At the conclusion of the postmortem, the lead investigator or his deputy can be fully briefed by the pathologist as to any findings.

It is important that the attending officer obtains the following samples from any honor killing postmortem:

- Anal, vaginal, oral swabs to assess whether any sexual assault has taken place and potentially link an offender to the offense.
- Fingernail scrapings: To determine if the victim had a chance to defend herself and if a suspect's DNA maybe evident.
- Head and pubic hair: Again to identify DNA evidence that might open up further lines of enquiry in identifying suspects or potential witnesses.
- Blood, urine, stomach contents: In HBV, family members may force the victim to drink alcohol, take drugs, or ingest other chemicals or for the victim to drink poisons.
- Pretransfusion blood: To identify any other alien toxins in the body that may support a prosecution case.

Postmortem Records

It is important that an accurate record of the postmortem is obtained. All of the injuries should be documented and photographed to allow interpretation by both the pathologist and lead investigator. By undertaking this, several things can be evidenced, such as predeath injuries, defense injuries, fatal injuries, postdeath injuries, assessment of the number and type of weapons causing injuries, determination if there was more than one assailant, and evidence of incapacitation. This information will not only aid the development of future lines of enquiry and support hypothesis generation, but can be revisited at a later date as further information becomes known or available.

Postmortem Photography

Photographs of postmortems are particularly useful as they can show the body in its original state of recovery. The photos should be taken with some form of size scale and should include both external and internal injuries. Frequently, victims of honor killings suffer a multitude of injuries, such as stab wounds. How the injuries are photographed should be a matter of discussion between the pathologist, lead investigator, and a photographer experienced in pathological photography.

Weapons

Where weapons have been found, it is good practice to show these to the pathologist after the postmortem so that he can provide an opinion as to whether the injuries suffered by the victim could have been caused by that weapon.

The reason for showing weapons *after* the postmortem is to prevent any future accusation of leading the pathologist findings during the postmortem.

In many honor killings where weapons are used, the force is often so extreme that weapons are damaged and broken. Again, the pathologist may be able to give an informed opinion as to what level of force was used on the victim and over what period.

Release of the Body

It is difficult to give guidance on the subject of releasing the body because this will be dictated by the respective legislative and working practices of individual jurisdictions. However, it is important that the body is not released until the requirements of the investigation have been met in respect to it, including confirmation of the victim's identity, all forensic tests and evidence collection is complete, and there is no need for any further postmortem examinations. The decision when to release a body, however, can be further complicated because many communities (and their religious beliefs) may have their grief compounded by the postmortem, and if the body cannot be released for a significant period of time. Ultimately, each case has to be treated on its own merits and decisions may be made from discussion between law enforcement, lawyers, specialist HBV nongovernmental organizations (NGOs), and relevant judicial authority cognizant of family wishes.

It is worth noting that the release of the body may be an issue in honor killing cases. Some families who are involved in the killing may not want the body to be returned to them. A lead investigator should consider whether this may add circumstantial evidence to the case and support an honor killing theory. How this evidence is adduced and introduced should be a discussion between law enforcement and prosecution lawyers.

Victims

In many HBV allegations, the victim is alive and, in this section, we consider the issues that secondary investigators need to consider when dealing with these victims.

Risk Assessment

Law enforcement needs to understand the risk of harm an HBV victim faces (as stated previously, this may be substantial) and how the risk is best managed. Therefore, risk assessment should be undertaken by law enforcement on first meeting an alleged victim of HBV. (The methods and processes of risk assessment and management are discussed in Chapter 7.)

Victim Age

Key to how cases are managed by the police, but also how legislation sees the investigation, will be the age of victim, whether a child or adult. (The role of children and HBV will be discussed in Chapter 10, but it is a significant and defining factor in police and partnership response.)

Medical Examination

Dependent on the allegation made by the victim, the age of the offense, and the willingness of the victim should be subject to a medical examination that may include a sexual assault examination as well. These examinations should be carried out by a suitably qualified practitioner in a suitable environment where the victim feels comfortable and where there is no possibility of cross contamination of forensic evidence. Where it is relevant, photographs should be taken of injuries, marks, and ripped clothing by qualified photographers so that the photos themselves can be presented as evidence in any future court trial. If the case involves a sexual offense allegation, the victim should be supported by a specially trained sexual offense investigation officer who also has knowledge, experience, and training in HBV issues.

Interviewing Victims of HBV

It is important that victims of HBV are interviewed by law enforcement in order to obtain as much information about the allegation as possible. The interview should take place as soon as is practicable and all HBV victim interviews should be visually recorded to aid in later interpretation of the interview, and also so that the evidence is available should something untoward happen to the victim. In some jurisdictions where victims are regarded as especially vulnerable and/or at risk, video-recorded interviews are admissible in court as evidence. Investigators should strongly consider this for HBV victims where possible, as it is not unknown for families to attempt to manipulate the evidence given by a victim, and attendance at court may increase the risk for the victim.

Where and how a victim is interviewed depends on many factors: the allegation being made, the age of the victim, the risk to her well being, the resources available to obtain an effective, admissible, and relevant interview, access to relevant support agencies (if appropriate), and the wishes of the victim herself.

HBV, as we have seen, presents many complexities and, as such, the use of appropriately skilled and knowledgeable interviewing officers for victims is of paramount importance. Therefore, we suggest that the interviewing officer has an awareness of, experience, and training in HBV matters. Dependent on the age of the victim and/or the crime being investigated, these officers also may need additional skills, e.g., interviewing children, interviewing victims of serious sexual assault, or even both.

The nature of the offenses that are being alleged is important and it is important that the investigating officer does not underestimate the seriousness of what victims tell them. Therefore, victims should always be believed regardless of how unbelievable an allegation may seem. We have seen that girls can be killed for being too *Westernized* or wearing makeup. It is important also to note that, at the time of presentation to law enforcement, specific offenses may not have taken place; however, victim's fear is often an accurate indicator of the likelihood of violent offenses. Investigators should take victim fear very seriously. In this regard, it is important to bear in mind the significant hurdles a potential victim will have had to negotiate in order to even bring her concerns to police attention. Indeed, alerting police can in itself be sufficient cause for HBV.

Consideration of a Victim's Wishes

The wishes of victims should always be considered when developing investigative strategies, but they should not be the major factor driving actions taken by law enforcement. These decisions should be taken on the basis of the seriousness of the offense, the risk faced by the victim, the age of the victim, the identification of potential future victims (i.e., siblings, cousins, etc.), and what is in the public interest. In some cases, this may mean that a victim's wishes may be overridden, for example, in a situation where a victim wished for law enforcement not to charge a family member with an HBV-related offense, but where there was a high-assessed risk of future harm to the victim or her siblings, the wishes of the victim would likely be overridden in the interests of preventing offending and protecting potential victims of crime. If actions are taken that are contrary to the victim's wishes, it is always best practice to inform the victim of the reasons why this is the case. It is also good practice to have available the support and guidance of specialist HBV services available that can advise and support the victim.

Victims Presenting Evidence in Court

Victims should always have confidence in the criminal justice system. This is particularly important in HBV cases as the mere fact that victims have entered this process could cost them their lives. Therefore, law enforcement should always consider the use of special measures for victims of HBV in court, such as video evidence in chief or enabling them to give evidence via video link. The application of "special measures" in court for HBV victims will depend on a particular jurisdiction's practices and procedures.

Witness Protection

Depending on the level of risk faced by some victims who have given evidence in court, some may need to enter Witness Protection Programs. We do not intend discussing the strategies and tactics of witness protection programs in this book because we do not wish to publicize these tactics and procedures. We suggest that discussions should be had with the law enforcement units that manage witness protection programs to discuss the most suitable strategies to implement. However, investigators should always be sensitive to what they are requiring of HBV victims when asking them to enter into a witness protection program. The victims will be moved away from their family, friends, community, and all that is familiar to them, and placed in an area and with people they do not know or possibly do not understand. Isolation is one of the biggest reasons why HBV victims return home after relocation despite the significant danger they may face.

Partner Agencies

An effective law enforcement response to HBV and engagement with victims can be enhanced by the relationship with and type of partner agency (statutory partners or specialist NGOs) support that is available. Any HBV investigation should always attempt to engage with other agencies with expertise in HBV so the victim is afforded the best possible care and support. As well as providing law enforcement with support and guidance, this also is likely to increase the victim's confidence in law enforcement actions.

Continued Engagement With Victims

Once a victim has contacted police, there should be continued engagement with her as this provides support for the victim and will help develop the relationship between the victim and law enforcement. This is likely to provide benefits for risk management (law enforcement will be able to monitor the victim's situation), it may encourage further revelations (if any) from the victim, allow the victim to be kept up to date with the investigation, and the victim can be prepared for any forthcoming court case. How contact with the victim is maintained and by whom will be determined by local policies governing such matters. We recommend, where available, that a family liaison officer (FLO) be appointed, and, if this is not possible, this role should be undertaken by the investigating officer himself. In addition, there are significant benefits for law enforcement in working with partner agencies to them in achieving their aims of continued contact with the victim. It is noteworthy also that, in order to protect the victim from potential harm, covert techniques and covert communication devices may need to be deployed to stay in contact with the victim. For obvious reasons, these tactics will not be discussed in a public arena, such as this book.

Uncooperative Victims

Law enforcement may, on occasion, face uncooperative victims. This can happen for many reasons; many of them related to the issues faced by victims in having to deal with law enforcement. These include isolation from family and friends, the potential criminalizing of their family, language barriers, cultural issues, the belief that law enforcement may actually support HBV practices, and fear concerning the ability of law enforcement to protect them. When faced with uncooperative victims, law enforcement should not just sit back and do nothing. A risk assessment should be completed and law enforcement should work with partners to implement a risk management strategy.

How law enforcement responds to unwilling victims depends upon the age of the victim. When the victim is a child, there may be legislation that can support in protecting the victim irrespective of the victim's cooperation. If the victim is an adult and uncooperative and where law enforcement has done everything in its power to intervene, it is important that all of its actions should be documented to provide a paper trail of law enforcement attempts to protect the victim. This means that, should the worst happen, law enforcement can go some way to defending its actions in light of any criticism from family, friends, communities, and the media. When faced with an uncooperative victim, at the very least, law enforcement should make it clear to the victim the level of risk she faces and advise her on risk management measures.

Witnesses

When investigating HBV, identifying credible and reliable witnesses can be extremely difficult especially where the potential key witnesses are family or community members. Any investigator speaking to potential witnesses must have an open mind and not hold any preconceptions about individuals. All witnesses should be treated with respect and dignity as this will have a significant effect on whether they cooperate with the investigation. Investigators also should ensure that they use appropriate and sensitive questioning to obtain the best possible evidence. There are a number of considerations for the investigator when speaking to witnesses; these include establishing what witnesses know, assessing their reliability, identifying if they have specific allegiances and where they lie, considering if they are acting under duress, assessing whether the witnesses are in danger, and considering if witnesses may be potential suspects. In this section, we consider the issues pertaining to witnesses in cases of HBV.

Identification of Witnesses

In any investigation, the investigator has to consider how he will identify witnesses, how he will make contact with witnesses, and how witness should be interviewed. To further complicate issues, some witnesses may be close family members of the victim, and the witnesses may be victims themselves or even potential suspects.

Identifying who the witnesses are will depend upon the crime allegation, where it happened, the context of the offense, and any historical events that have led to the primary offense. In the list below, we detail likely witnesses in HBV cases:

- Family members, both immediate and extended
- Partners of victims, be they known to the family or concealed by the victim from the family
- Colleagues, at school, college, university, or work (including peers and supervisors)
- Teachers, lecturers, or other academic professionals who have regular contact with the victim
- Friends identified by both the victim and family or by mutual friends of the victim
- Professional personnel, such as medical, social services, local authority, legal
- Nongovernment agencies, e.g., outreach workers
- Independent witnesses who are not known personally to the victim, but may have witnessed the relevant crime or previous crimes
- Witnesses who may be identified by implementation of various appeal strategies, such as door-to-door enquiries, media appeals, CCTV examination.

Contacting Witnesses

Within any investigation, contacting some witnesses will be easier and safer than contacting others. This is particularly important in cases of HBV because the fact that police have made contact may place an individual in significant danger. Therefore, it is important that there is a clear strategy concerning how, when, and where law enforcement will contact witnesses. Engaging partner agencies to make contact with potential witnesses also may be a useful tactic to consider when approaching particularly vulnerable HBV witnesses.

Risk Assessment of Witnesses

Each witness should be subject to a risk assessment to determine the risk of harm he/she faces from law enforcement contact and to set a contact strategy for the witness that is based upon the assessed risk. Dependent upon the risk level, the means of contacting witnesses in HBV cases can vary from direct approaches made away from family/community members to indirect approaches through other professionals, such as medical staff, teachers, work colleagues, and outreach workers. Again, this list is not inclusive, but is used to highlight that a partnership approach between police and other agencies is both a safe and effective way of contacting witnesses.

The risk faced by witnesses also may affect the information they provide, which can be tainted and, at worst, wholly inaccurate in an attempt to derail any enquiry. There may be many reasons for this, such as fear of reprisals, fear of court, protecting assailants, or distrust of law enforcement.

As well as taking statements from witnesses at the scenes, investigating officers need to consider their proximity to an offense and whether there is any forensic value in forensically examining their clothes and property or obtaining photos of the victim. The witness may have recorded the incident on a phone or other data device and, if this is the case, efforts should be made to persuade the witness to hand the device to police for examination. If this is refused, then other arrangements should be made to obtain the data from the device at the earliest opportunity.

Categorizing Witnesses

It is useful to categorize witnesses at the earliest opportunity because this facilitates the design of appropriate witness management strategies. It is useful to do this based on the witnesses' relationship to the offense, the victim, the family, and the risk that they face. This decision and rationale for the categorization of a witness should be clearly documented so that decision making is clear and any later challenge can be defended. A useful system has been produced in the United Kingdom that aids in witness classification and we reproduce it below. Within this system there are three broad classes of witness: the *vulnerable, intimidated,* and *significant witness.*

- *Vulnerable witnesses* are individuals who demonstrate a degree of vulnerability that may impact upon the reliability of their evidence. Examples of vulnerable individuals include children, those suffering from mental health or other significant impairment of intelligence or social functioning, and a significant physical disorder or disability. Typically, it is best practice for specially trained officers to engage with vulnerable witnesses, e.g., specially trained children interviewers or those with experience of working with particular vulnerable groups.

- *Intimidated witnesses* are those who give information under duress because they are in fear of harm to themselves or other loved ones or who may be supportive of HBV practices because of pressure placed on them by their community, family, and friends. The level of intimidation witnesses experience can be classified as below and this will determine the extent to which various witness management processes are enacted and the veracity of the information provided:
  - Life threatening, where witnesses are judged to be at risk of death as a result of their involvement as a witness
  - Nonlife threatening, but serious intimidation
  - Low-level intimidation/harassment
  - Fear of low-level intimidation and harassment where the individual is fearful
  - Fear of court and judicial procedure where an individual fears the court process
- *Significant witnesses* include those witnesses who have directly seen or heard an offense(s). Significant witnesses will vary in the level of risk they face: Some may be bystanders with no links to the victim, her family, or community, and their involvement may present them with few risks of harm. Conversely, other witnesses may also fall into the vulnerable and intimidated witness categories.

It is important to note that some witnesses will face a low risk of harm or intimidation even though they may be classified as a significant witness and may be happy to provide information to police. Similarly, there may be witnesses who also face a low risk of harm and can provide valuable information to the inquiry. Witnesses of this sort often have no direct relationship with or link to the victim, her family, or community. For these witnesses, there is likely to be no identified risk in contacting them. In these circumstances, there will be no need to devise special strategies and, thus, the usual approach taken by law enforcement in seeking assistance and statements will suffice. For other types of witnesses, consideration may need to be made as to how to approach them. This might be through liaison with other agencies and information may need to be obtained from the witness using specially trained investigators and special measures, such as video recorded interviews.

Reluctant Witnesses

One feature of HBV crimes is the reluctance of some witnesses to engage with law enforcement. Investigators should endeavor to talk to reluctant witness about the case in an attempt to reconcile their concerns and obtain evidence. Reluctant witnesses should generally not be forced to provide evidence because this can have a wide ranging effect, not only on the present case, but future cases and community confidence in the police. Working with key partners can be an effective way of working with reluctant witnesses. Partners, such as HBV and other domestic violence charities, may provide advice and/or support for reluctant witnesses that may be helpful in obtaining their cooperation. Prosecutors should be made aware at the earliest opportunity of reluctant witnesses so that a decision can be made as to how they can be effectively managed within the overall criminal justice process.

Hostile Witnesses

Within HBV offenses, there also may be a number of hostile witnesses, individuals who may have important information, but who may be opposed to the investigative process. How hostile witnesses are managed will depend on local protocols, discussion with the relevant prosecutors, and the investigative aims. Contact and interaction with hostile witnesses should always be recorded by law enforcement.

Interviewing Witnesses

Where a witness has been designated as *significant, vulnerable,* or *intimidated,* we recommend that, where possible, these witnesses are interviewed by law enforcement. It is acknowledged, of course, that this may prove difficult, particularly in the case of intimidated witnesses who may be reluctant to attend an interview and, thus, where an interview is refused, officers should still attempt to make some record of the witness's evidence. Interviewing is recommended because taking a statement necessarily constricts the information provided by the witness to the questions asked by the statement taker and may force the witness to self-edit his/her information and/or fail to provide other relevant information (Roberts and Herrington, 2011). A well-planned interview allows the witness the opportunity to expand on information with the possibility that a richer account is provided. This is clearly an advantage for significant witnesses who may hold valuable information to progress an investigation.

When a witness has been categorized and designated for interview, investigators should devise an interview strategy so that best evidence can be achieved from that witness. An interview strategy should be a written document that sets out clearly the aims, objectives, and methods to be used in the interview. At a minimum, an interview strategy should contain:

- Aims and objectives for the interview: This consists of clearly identifying and articulating what the interview is trying to achieve. Aims and objectives will be identified from a consideration of the present state of the investigation and will include what facts are presently known and what is unknown. There are many reasons for interviewing a witness and space prevents producing an exhaustive list, but, as examples, the objective of an interview might be to obtain an account of events, to question further or challenge a previous witness account, to obtain information about a victim or suspect, or to obtain information to carry out a full risk assessment. A clear statement of the aims and objectives of an interview allows judgments to be made regarding the quality of the interview—the extent to which aims and objectives were achieved—and may inform subsequent investigative decisions, such as whether to interview another individual.
- Interview topics: This should be a statement of what topics will be included in the interview and the order that the topics will be approached. Topics might include background information on the witness, victim, suspect, or the family, details of what the witness saw, historical information, etc. The order topics are dealt with can be significant in an interview. Some topics are highly emotive and are best considered after rapport has been developed with a witness rather than at the start of an interview. Likewise, some topics may be of limited importance for a particular interview.
- Questions: Consideration should be given to the type and nature of questions that will be asked of witnesses. In general, open, non-leading questions are preferable as these lead to fuller accounts and greater information retrieval.
- Selection of interviewers: Who should carry out the interview? Interviewers with HBV awareness would be beneficial and, if not available, a briefing of the officers concerning HBV should be considered.
- Location of interviews: Where the interview should take place is important especially for intimidated witnesses and consideration should be given as to whether it will occur in a law enforcement office or other location. This will be influenced by the risk assessment of a particular witness.
- Briefing interviewers: Every HBV case has its own individual features; therefore, interviewing officers should be made aware of the current state of the investigation and the information known to date.

- Debriefing interviewers so that information obtained from an interview can be passed quickly in to the enquiry, the lead investigator, and to other officers.
- Supplementary interviews: Information given by witnesses can change for many reasons, which, in turn, may necessitate further interviews. If this is the case, consideration should be given as to whether subsequent interviews are in the best interests of the witness and/or the enquiry and should be done in consultation with prosecution lawyers.

Interview Advisors

Where an investigation is particularly serious or complex, a lead investigator may consider deploying a specialist interview advisor who can provide an informed and professional over-arching interview strategy. This is a specific role in some legislatures, such as the United Kingdom. When interview advisors are available, they can manage all facets of the witness interview process, working closely with the lead investigator allowing the lead investigator to manage and oversee other investigative areas.

Witnesses Who Become Suspects

There is a significant possibility that a witness could become a suspect. The investigating officer needs to, as far as practicable, give consideration to this when planning interviews. This should entail interviewers being properly briefed so that they can respond appropriately where a confession is received or the information being given by the interviewee is such that he should be treated as a suspect in accordance with the jurisdiction of that area. Any decision made around the appropriateness of the course of action will depend on the seriousness of the crime being investigated, the role the witness had in the perpetration of that crime, and his actual involvement. It may be that the interview is suspended and advice is taken from a more senior officer or the lead investigator.

Witnesses Giving Evidence at Court

Law enforcement should consider and address the needs of witnesses who will give evidence in a court trial as part of any witness strategy. Like victims, most witnesses find giving evidence at trial daunting, stressful, and frightening. In HBV cases, this may be compounded where individuals are giving evidence against family members. It is important that witnesses are kept up to date with the enquiry and the progress of the case. We cannot over-emphasize the support that partner agencies, notably HBV specific

NGOs, can provide in this process. In certain cases, a specific police officer, as a named point of contact, may be the way forward especially in a serious or complex enquiry involving many officers. The key aim for police in working with witnesses has to be, as much as possible, the removal of anxiety, the reduction of frustration, and the removal of hostility.

Suspects

The effective identification, arrest, and interview of suspects are paramount in any HBV investigation if it is to succeed in the criminal justice arena. However, given the complexities of family and community dynamics, even though the suspects may be known, arrest and interview may not be the most appropriate way forward in every investigation. In this section, we consider the issue for the secondary investigator in dealing with HBV suspects.

Decision to Arrest

Any decision to arrest or not to arrest should be made by a senior officer or lead investigator who has a significant knowledge and experience of HBV issues. We suggest that, where appropriate, these decisions are taken in partnership with both statutory and nonstatutory agencies so that decisions can be made that are in the best interests of the victim, family, community, and public at large. There may be no right or wrong decision in these circumstances, but we advise that, whatever decision is made, this is recorded along with the rationale for the decision and who was consulted in making it.

In jurisdictions like the United Kingdom,* where the arrest of suspects forms part of the evidence collection phase of an investigation, it is likely that an investigator will arrest a suspect for the more serious allegations or where there is a significant risk of future violence.

In some circumstances, a decision not to arrest may be made. Typically, these circumstances involve combinations of situations where the allegations are at a relatively low level (e.g., minor harassment, restrictions of movement or lifestyle) where there is no other evidence available than that provided by the victim herself or where victims may not wish to commit their allegation in an admissible format, where it is felt that risks of harm are low and can be managed by other means, and/or where it is felt that to implement an arrest and interview may place individuals at further risk of harm. In these circumstances,

---

* Of course, in other jurisdictions, the decision to arrest a suspect will depend upon local legislation.

the future safety of the victim is paramount and liaison with other agencies in designing and implementing intervention strategies is strongly recommended.

Where a decision is made to arrest, investigators will need to consider and implement arrest, interview, and charging strategies as well as liaison with prosecution agents. We consider these issues in the sections below.

Communication Strategy

Where HBV enquiries are undertaken, communication is paramount with victims, witnesses, affected families, communities, and all relevant partners. If this is not undertaken, this may create concern within the community and may affect the confidence it has in law enforcement. We, therefore, recommend that, when planning an arrest for HBV, law enforcement should develop a communication strategy to explain the situation to the wider public through the media and via community contacts. This will help the public understand not only what has happened but why it has happened. This is especially important in cases where early arrests are made. (We discuss the development of communication strategies in Chapter 9.)

Arrest Strategy

Once a suspect is identified, the decision to arrest should always be made with careful consideration and planning because this may have serious ramifications not only for the prosecution case but also for family and community confidence in the police. Cultural issues and differences should not be a barrier to arresting suspects, but they will be a significant consideration. Once again, advice and guidance may be obtained from HBV specialists and other partners concerning these matters. However, where a quick arrest is essential to save life, or prevent the escape of an offender, investigating officers may not always have the opportunity to consult with partners prior to arrest. The safety of individuals and the community must come first and then the interests of justice must follow.

Implementing an arrest strategy for an HBV perpetrator should be no different with respect to general law enforcement actions than arrests for any offense. In any arrest, investigators will need to consider their power of arrest, any intelligence that informs the arrest decision, the identity of suspects, their location, other relevant addresses, and vehicles they have access to, the timing of the arrest, and searches of the suspects property. There should be an arrest plan, prearrest briefing, and the custody procedures and processes. Careful consideration should be given as to how the arrest will take place given the likelihood the suspect will be a family member and the arrest could well take place in the home of both victim and suspect.

Where there is more than one arrest required, arrest strategies need to consider how the arrests should be coordinated and where the detainees will be taken, e.g., are they to be taken to different custody locations? If there are multiple arrests, or the case is high profile, alerting custody managers and senior officers of imminent arrests is advisable so that they can prepare their stations and staff and have appropriate strategies put in place to deal with any community and media interest.

Any arrest at a suspect's home address carries with it a certain amount of risk and arresting officers should consider how many people are likely to be present or near to the family address at the time of the arrest. It may be necessary to take control of premises and, therefore, sufficient resources will need to be deployed to not only carry out the arrest but also to safely secure the premises. If there is a credible belief that the premises may have been the site of a crime or it is believed that exhibits pertinent to the crime(s) being investigated are located at the scene, there will be a need to arrange for forensic analysis.

Arrest Strategy, Staff Requirements

For a planned arrest and within the arrest strategy, consideration should be given to deploying:

- Officers to carry out the arrest and, where there are multiple arrests to be made, different arrest teams. It may be appropriate for multiple arrests to have an arrest coordinator.
- Exhibits officer and crime scene investigator for each location.
- Transportation for officers and suspects.
- An interpreter where language may be an issue.
- Support individuals where suspects are children or juveniles in line with legislative practices for that jurisdiction.
- Cordon/scene security officer(s).
- Specialist equipment to secure entry.
- Video/camera equipment to record any subsequent arrest and search if considered useful or appropriate.
- Community leaders or HBV NGO services to provide community reassurance and reduce community impact. However, the information given to these individuals should be limited dependent on how well known and trusted they are to the investigating officers.

Briefing Arresting Officers

Any arresting officers should be fully briefed as to what their roles are, the issues of HBV, and the aim of the arrest operation. Clear instructions should be given to arrest and search teams and these instructions should be documented. It may be appropriate to have relevant partners and community leaders present at these briefings to provide community reassurance.

Suspect Custody

Once a suspect is in custody, his detention will be controlled in relation to the legislation of that jurisdiction. If a case is particularly complex or involves multiple suspects, a dedicated custody management officer may need to be appointed so that all issues are managed effectively.

Collection of Material From Suspects

It is important for investigators to ensure that relevant evidence is obtained from suspects (the procedures governing collection of these will be determined by local law and protocols). Material collected might include:

- Appropriate samples, such as nail clippings, fingerprints, swabs (hands, mouth, penile, vaginal, anal, or other as appropriate to the case in question), samples obtained (saliva, blood, urine)
- Photographs taken including face, full body in different profiles, injuries, and other areas as dictated by the investigating officer
- Examination by a suitably qualified medical practitioner particularly if injuries noted so that an opinion can be obtained as to how those injuries may have occurred
- Seizing of clothing and footwear

Debrief of Arresting Officers

It is important that arresting officers are debriefed at the earliest opportunity so that any significant comments or statements made by a suspect are captured. These comments will be essential in the interview phase of the arrest strategy.

Suspect Interviews

Information provided by suspects may be vital to the investigation. Given the complexities of the HBV investigations and the potential for many suspects, a coherent and detailed interview strategy should be developed prior to an arrest. The lead investigator should play a significant part in this process and, if available, an interview advisor should be deployed, particularly where multiple interviews are taking place at the same time.

Selection of Interviewers

With any HBV cases, a key strategic issue will be the selection of interviewers. They should be experienced and have knowledge and experience of HBV cases. When selecting interviewers, a team of two officers per suspect should be considered, with different officers for each suspect.

Briefing Interviewers

The interviewers should be briefed by the lead investigator so that they are aware of the case and the aims of the investigation. Interviewing officers should be aware of their role at an early stage so that they can prepare for any interview.

Interviewer Access to Lead Investigator

Interviewing officers should have access to the lead investigating officer both in the planning stage and during the interview so that notable updates can be passed quickly to the lead investigator and, if necessary, these can be disseminated to other interview teams or general enquiry teams, if appropriate.

Debrief of Interviewers

At the conclusion of the interview process, interviewers should be debriefed at the earliest opportunity to establish what information has been obtained, how the account fits in with other known evidence, whether any further investigation action needs to take place, and what further enquiries need to be made.

Interview Strategy

In designing an interview strategy, it is important to consider the objectives of the interview. As detailed in relation to witnesses, a clear statement of the aims and objectives of an interview allow interviewers and other investigators the opportunity to evaluate the quality of their interview. The *PEACE* interview structure is advised as the most appropriate interview structure. This emphasizes appropriate planning (P) of the interview; detailed explanation (E) of what the suspect should expect and the development of rapport throughout the interview; obtaining the account (A) using an appropriate interview approach, such as *conversation management* (see Interview Tactics below); closure (C) of the interview in which the suspect is given sufficient information to enable him to understand what the outcomes of the interview will be; and the product of the interview is finally evaluated (E) by the interviewers and senior investigators to determine future directions.

Interviewers need to be aware that, just as with witnesses, suspects may present with a range of attitudes toward the interviewers, such as compliance at one extreme through to hostility at the other. Regardless of the demeanor of the suspect, interviewers should carry out the interview in a professional manner giving due respect to the suspect. Demonstrations of anger, threats, or other aggressive tactics by the interviewers will not be productive because these will serve to alienate the suspect and may have a negative impact upon community relations. Likewise, interruptions of suspects should be minimized as should signs that the interviewers are not listening or engaged with what the suspect is saying as these tend to alienate the suspect and act as barriers to communication.

Rapport-Based Interviews

The most useful approach to take with HBV suspects as with witnesses is one based on the development of rapport in which the suspect is able to express his views and feelings and where interviewers listen carefully to what is said. Many suspects feel justified in their actions and some are proud of what they have done, and this approach allows such individuals the opportunity to express their views, which often leads to admissions. Similarly, some suspects, after committing an HBV offense, will feel some guilt and remorse. Frequently these individuals have injured a daughter or son and, on reflection, the enormity of what they have done occurs to them. Again, a rapport-based approach is most likely to allow these individuals the opportunity to unburden themselves.

Interview Tactics

As regards interview tactics, conversation management (Shepherd, 1993) is recommended. Here suspects are given an initial opportunity to express their version of events and to present anything that they deem relevant (suspect agenda) with minimal interruption from the interviewers. This usually follows an initial open question that asks the suspect to detail any knowledge he has about the event. When the suspect has completed his agenda, the interview moves into a clarification phase where the suspect's account is clarified by the interviewers. The police agenda then follows in which interviewers explore topics that are of interest to them, but have not so far been considered. Finally, the challenge phase occurs in which interviewers challenge the suspect's account utilizing evidence.

Interview Topics

As with witness interviews, in planning the suspect interview strategy, it is vital for interviewers to clearly identify those topics of interest to them, to be completely conversant with all aspects of the investigation of relevance to the interview, and to clearly identify the challenges that they can put to the suspect. There is a great deal of literature to aid police in preparing interview strategies (Roberts and Herrington, 2011).

Charging Suspects

Once the investigators or lead investigator feels they have sufficient evidence for a suspect to be charged, then, in line with the legislation of that area, they should be charged with the relevant offenses and brought to the appropriate court. The decision to charge and the offenses to be charged will often be made in discussion with and authorized by the relevant prosecution agency. The role of prosecution agencies will be subject to a separate chapter in this book (see Chapter 6).

If it is felt there is insufficient evidence to charge a suspect, considerations relating to the risks faced by the victim, witnesses, and the suspect will all have to be considered by the investigating officer. Risk management is then the priority and this is discussed in Chapter 7.

Overseas Offenses

In honor killings and other HBV offenses, victims may be taken away from their country of residence or origin in an attempt to evade the jurisdiction of their "home" nation. The law enforcement investigation, therefore, will have to take place with the appropriate International Letters of Request between the relevant prosecution agencies and central government agencies. Advice should be sought from local prosecution agencies to seek the most appropriate way forward in any state-to-state investigative cooperation.

Use of Interpreters

A significant number of HBV victims, witnesses, or suspects may need to use an interpreter when they liaise with law enforcement or other agency. It is important that an officially recognized interpreter is used to ensure the integrity of the information that is provided. Under *no circumstances* should law enforcement consider using family members or children as interpreters. It is also the case that some interpreters are known to the family and the community and will misinterpret interviewee accounts to protect the guilty, protect the community, and to show their commitment to honor issues.

Where it is suspected that an interpreter is misinterpreting an account, this should be challenged through the appropriate channels, the interpreter removed from the interview, and a new interpreter sought. The integrity of an official interpreter will always be higher than one that is not officially recognized.

Conclusions

In this chapter, we have considered some of the issues in the secondary investigation of HBV offenses. Throughout, we have noted the importance of careful planning of strategies to maximize evidence collection and information from victims, witnesses, and suspects. We also have stressed the importance of sensitivity to the risks faced by victims and witnesses. In the next chapter, we move on to consider the issues that are presented by particular forms of HBV and the related considerations for investigators.

Effective Investigation of Honor-Based Violence 3

5

Secondary Investigation, Issues With Offense Types

In this chapter, we discuss some of the pertinent issues associated with the secondary investigation of specific offenses that may form part of honor-based violence (HBV). This will not be a specific guide to investigation of these offenses per se, as that is beyond the scope of this book. However, the aim is to highlight to the reader some of the unique conditions that may exist when HBV is an issue. We do not intend to repeat what has already been written in this book, but this section should arm the reader with additional tools and knowledge specific to individual offenses.

Homicide

The investigation of homicide itself presents unique challenges to investigating officers, and these challenges can be compounded with honor killings. When investigating honor killings, the building block principles discussed in earlier chapters should be rigorously followed to ensure a full and comprehensive investigation.

Key factors to consider when investigating honor killings include:

- The conspiracy to kill: Honor killings are rarely spontaneous acts, but are an organized and premeditated offense. Therefore, it is essential that the investigating team not only identify the principle assailants, but also those that have conspired to murder. The conspiracy may have taken place locally, across regions, or across national boundaries.
- How the victim has died, where, and when:
  - The body deposition site for an honor killing is not always the attack site. Therefore, it is incumbent on the investigation team to identify the attack site, how the body was transferred to the deposition site, and by whom.
  - There may be some considerable time between the death of the victim and the finding of the body; therefore, it is important that, as far as possible, a time of death is established.

- Prior to the killing, the victim is often imprisoned and may have even been kidnapped. If this is the case, then the investigation team will need to establish where the victims were held, and there may have been more than one location. Also, the site of imprisonment may not have been the attack site. How the victim was moved around is also important if that is the case.

- Honor killing victims may have experienced extensive physical and sexual abuse both prior to death and even postdeath. Therefore, it is essential at any postmortem that these issues are discussed with the pathologist.

- Victimology of the victim is important to identify both a motive and likely suspects in respect to an honor killing. By finding out how the victim lived, there is significant potential to establish how she died. The investigating teams should consider speaking to family members, community members, friends, acquaintances, peers, work/education colleagues, professionals who have had association with the victim, and looking at the victim's social media sites.

- Suspicious suicides and/or suspicious deaths: As we have discussed already, many homicide suspects will attempt to conceal a homicide by making it look like a suicide or an accident (for example, a road traffic accident or house fire). If there are any suspicions as to the veracity of a death and where HBV may be an issue, then we recommend treating the matter as a homicide until the matter is proved conclusively that it is, in fact, a suicide. Key evidence in assisting investigating officers to make a decision may come from undertaking a victimology investigation as detailed above.

- We are aware that some honor killing victims will be moved from their country of residence and taken abroad where they will be killed. They are often taken to countries and areas that are sympathetic to honor killings or where it is known that there will not be an effective investigation. These type of investigations can prove to be extremely problematic and the success will be dependent on nation-to-nation assistance, what charges can be proved within the home jurisdiction (i.e., conspiracy offenses), and whether the victim and suspect are nationals of the investigating area (e.g., a U.K. national who murders another U.K. national overseas can face trial in the United Kingdom).

Sexual Offenses

Sexual assaults are a common feature of HBV and this is often used to dominate and humiliate the victim. HBV victims can be subjected to repeated rapes especially following a forced marriage. Similarly, in honor killings, victims may be raped as part of an attack. It, therefore, is essential that any investigating officer considers the following when investigating sexual assault where HBV is suspected:

- Establish the age of the victim, lest she be under the age of consent.
- The validity of the marriage should forced marriage be suspected.
- Whether the victim consented to the marriage.
- Where the marriage took place; there may be other offenses to consider, such as child trafficking if a child was taken abroad to be forced into marriage and then raped.
- How and when sexual assault started.
- Were sexual assaults committed overseas or did they start within the investigating officer's jurisdiction.
- What other violence or restraint was used in the commission of a sexual assault.
- Sensitively undertakes the difficult task of obtaining samples and swabs from the victim to prove intercourse, rape, and any other offense.

Another feature of rape with respect to HBV is that if an individual is raped by another then that also may bring shame onto a family, resulting in the family undertaking criminal actions to restore their family honor. This can mean killing their family member or forcing the victim of the rape to marry her attacker to restore the family honor. These are issues that the investigating officer should consider in gathering evidence to prove sexual offenses.

Domestic Violence

Domestic violence, such as physical and emotional abuse, is commonly associated with HBV. One feature of domestic violence where HBV is involved is that different individuals may be responsible for it, dependent upon the marital status of the victim. Prior to a marriage, the perpetrator(s) are most likely to come from the victim's immediate family, such as parents and/or siblings, and, following a marriage, the abuse is most likely to be perpetrated by the husband and his family.

Therefore, it is essential for any investigating officer when dealing with domestic violence cases to consider whether HBV may be an issue. This should be done by appropriate and sensitive questioning of the victim. The investigating officer, however, should not automatically form the opinion that HBV is an issue based solely on ethnicity or religion.

If there is evidence that HBV is an issue, then the investigating officer needs to complete a comprehensive and detailed risk assessment and management process, engage with partners, and obtain evidence of criminal offenses. Any actions undertaken should be geared to protecting the victim or any other person near to the victim who may be at risk. The investigating officer should be aware that domestic violence and HBV are a volatile mixture with significant risk and investigative complexities.

Both actual and the threat of physical and psychological assaults are a key feature of HBV. Frequently, these are used as a means of controlling and exerting power over the victim. As with any assault, it is important that the investigating officer details and catalogs the assault in question. It is important to remember, however, that, with respect to HBV, such assaults rarely happen in isolation and there may be evidence of a pattern of assault over time. The assaults may also be committed by many people, such as parents, siblings, cousins, uncles, aunts, husband, in-laws, or other extended family members as well as male members of the wider community. It is imperative that the investigating officer:

- Identifies as many incidents as possible because it is extremely rare that the assault will be an isolated incident.
- Identifies the assailant or assailants.
- Identifies witnesses, be they direct (having seen the assaults or seen injuries following assaults) or indirect (having heard the victim talk about the assaults).
- Identifies other corroborative evidence, such as photographs, recorded entries in diaries, social media, or disclosure by the victim to professional bodies, e.g., social services, teachers, medical professionals.
- Identifies that, in some jurisdictions, it is an offense to commit psychiatric or psychological assault and, therefore, evidence should be sought from medical professionals to prove this fact in a court of law.

Threats

Where threats to an individual's life or threats to cause serious harm are made within an HBV context, they should be taken extremely seriously. Therefore, all reasonable steps to protect individuals should be taken.

If a real and credible threat is received, then we recommend that the investigation is overseen by a senior manager within the police to ensure that an appropriate and proportionate response is forthcoming.

An investigating officer should consider the following points: how was the threat was received by police, and did it arise from collecting evidence or an intelligence route? Once the veracity of the source of the threats is confirmed, the way a threat is dealt with should follow a logical path:

- Assessment of the nature and severity of the threat: This should include a comprehensive risk assessment as discussed in Chapter 7.
- Response to mitigate the threat: This will include devising and implementing strategies that may be preventative or disruptive dependent on the information at hand and the willingness of the potential victim to cooperate.
- The resolution of the threat if at all possible. With HBV cases, this threat may last for the rest of the victim's life.

As with all risk assessment processes, the threat assessment is a dynamic process and should be constantly reviewed as new information comes to light.

In addition to any HBV risk assessment completed by the investigating officer, the following additional questions should be considered to assess the specific threat to life/threat of serious injury:

- How long has the information been in existence?
- Is the victim(s) identifiable and contactable?
- Can a venue for any potential attack be identified? It should be remembered (as discussed above) that this location could well be abroad, making the management of the threat potentially very difficult.
- What is the timescale of the attack and is it dependent on another event? The threats may be linked to other HBV issues, such as a victim participating in a forced marriage.
- Has the intelligence received been effectively evaluated and is the person who is providing the intelligence also at risk.
- What is the capability and capacity for the suspect(s) to carry out the threat? With respect to HBV cases, the investigating should not reduce the risk on the basis that the suspect is not known to police or because of his age. As we have already discussed, families are not averse to using young males to commit the most heinous of crimes in the name of honor
- Does the suspect intend to carry out the threat? Has there been a family council that has decided on the punishment the victim should receive?

In deciding on the level of threat, the senior investigating officer will then have to decide on the most effective response to prevent harm coming to individuals and also to gather sufficient evidence whereby suspects can be held to account, if that is appropriate.

As with previous topics discussed where proactive tactics will be used, we do not intend discussing law enforcement methodology in this book suffice to say advice should be sought from specialists about the tactics available to remove or reduce the risk in cases such as these. Whatever tactics used, they should be linked back to the wider risk assessment and strategy.

A decision that will need to be made is whether the victim should be warned as to the threat. There is no right or wrong answer, but it should be considered on a case-by-case basis. We would recommend, where at all possible, that the victim(s) be told and the risks managed. We would advocate the use of a FLO (family liaison officer) or other like officer to remain engaged with the victim so that there is a specific police point of contact that can build up information, intelligence, and evidence in respect to the victim's lifestyle and feed this into the risk management process.

Where there is a credible and real threat to a victim, then the investigating officer or FLO, if appointed, should consider gathering recent photographs of the victim, fingerprints, DNA, and any other identification data. This is done so that if the victim is killed, she can be identified using this information. There are facilities in the United Kingdom where this information can be stored and searched on a retrievable database.

Kidnapping

Many HBV offenses can be preempted by a kidnapping. Therefore, it is essential that, if a secondary investigating officer is given information that an HBV victim has been kidnapped, then this should be treated very seriously. The aim should be the safe return of the individual before she comes to any serious harm. Secondary to this should be the gathering of evidence to effect a successful prosecution.

In HBV, kidnap victims can be seriously harmed, killed, or removed from the country; therefore, the investigating officer should utilize all available resources to locate and rescue the victim. There are significant covert resources that can assist an investigating officer in locating a victim and return her to safety. Again, this is not the medium to openly discuss law enforcement's covert tactics and resources available to assist in this type of enquiry. Suffice it to say, officers should liaise with their specialist departments that can assist in this part of an investigation.

With respect to evidence gathering, the investigating officer should consider:

- Where the information has come from that the victim has been kidnapped. This information should be assessed as to its veracity.
- Who saw the kidnapping and what other evidence is available to prove the kidnapping, e.g., CCTV, eyewitnesses?

- Were any motor vehicles involved? If so, what type of vehicle (e.g., make, model, color), registration numbers/license number, direction of travel.
- Are any suspects known and what is known about the suspects (e.g. home address, premises to which they have access, vehicles they use, etc.)? When were they last seen and by whom? Do they have telephones and, if so, what numbers?

The key for the investigating officer is to build an intelligence picture around location of the kidnapping, victim, suspects, and vehicles. This will then drive a line of enquiry and prioritize actions to successfully rescue the victim.

Where things can get difficult for the victim and the investigating officer is where the victim may have already been taken out of the country. It should be noted that the investigating officer should not stop his investigation within his own jurisdiction until it is proved beyond doubt that the victim is out of the country. Even then, there is still scope to gather sufficient evidence to arrest and hold to account offenders who are still within his jurisdiction

False Imprisonment

Another common facet of HBV is false imprisonment. HBV victims are often held against their will as means of punishing perceived dishonorable behavior or as a prelude to more serious offenses committed against them. It is incumbent on the investigating officer to first rescue the victim from her imprisonment if this is ongoing. Similar covert techniques briefly mentioned above may be utilized in this situation.

Where the false imprisonment is no longer in action, evidence should be sought from witness testimony and, if the place of false imprisonment is identified, then from effective crime scene management and forensics. These crime scenes should be examined in accordance with local forensic procedures and with a consideration to the points made in the previous chapter.

Female Genital Mutilation (FGM) Offenses

There are a number of indicators that may highlight to law enforcement or other agencies that a girl may be at risk of FGM. These include:

- Any girl born to a mother who has been subjected to FGM.
- Any girl who has had a sibling subjected to FGM.
- Any girl withdrawn from personal, social, or health education as her family may not want the girl aware of her body and her rights. Girls

often do not know they are going to be subjected to FGM until the actual operation.

- Unexplained absences from school and following school holidays when the child may be taken abroad to be subjected to FGM; this allows for healing time before returning to her studies.
- When it is known an older female relative has travelled from the motherland to the girl's home.
- The girl herself may confide to others about a procedure.
- The girl may alert a teacher or another adult if she is aware of what is coming.
- The parents state that the girl will be taken out of the country for a prolonged period.
- The girl may talk about a prolonged visit to her country of origin or another FGM practicing country.
- Level of integration of a family into the adopted country's culture. Where there is little integration, this raises the risk of FGM when associated with other factors listed here.

FGM most often involves young children, and so the first priority for the investigating officer where FGM is suspected is the protection of the child. Officers, therefore, should consider the use of local child protection powers. The welfare of other children within the family, in particular, female siblings, should be reviewed as well.

The investigation should be the subject of regular, ongoing, multiagency reviews, the protocols for which are discussed in Chapter 10, to consider any further protective steps that need to be taken with regard to that child and any other siblings.

The child should be interviewed by a specialist trained officer, who is skilled and experienced in interviewing children, to obtain the best possible evidence for use in any prosecution. Additionally, information gained from the interview process will enable a risk assessment to be conducted as to the risk to any other children/siblings.

Corroborative evidence should be sought through a medical examination conducted by a qualified pediatrician. If the child refuses to be interviewed or undergo medical examination, the investigating officer should consider seeking assistance from partner agencies. Where consent for a medical examination is refused by a parent/guardian, then the investigating officer should consider using relevant legislation to obtain authority to undertake an examination.

Experience has shown us that, if there is any delay in FGM investigations, this can be damaging to the victim. It also increases the risk of her being pressured by family and her community into noncooperation with authorities. As such, early consultation between law enforcement and prosecutors (along with other statutory child protection partners) should be considered essential in bringing FGM cases to justice.

Investigating officers also should consider an effective strategy that should identify "excisors" (people who carry out FGM for payment or otherwise), and scenes of FGM operations. In identifying these, there is a potential to identify further victims and of closing down FGM networks.

If an investigating officer becomes aware of an adult female who has undergone FGM, then a full risk assessment should be conducted to assess the risk to her. Contact with partner agencies should be made as well so that any risks to other girls within the family (and extended family) can be considered.

Stalking and Harassment

A common feature of HBV is that victims are often followed and watched by family members, particularly if the family believes that they are transgressing family honor codes. Females are often policed by male members of their family or community and they may experience this from an early age. Any perceived transgression in their behavior will be reported back to senior male family members to consider what action is to be taken. The punishment for any transgression can be severe, such as beatings, false imprisonment, and even death.

Any law enforcement officer or staff member faced with a victim stating she was being followed, monitored, stalked, or harassed by male members of her family or community should take this allegation very seriously. Through appropriate and sensitive questioning, the officer should establish the full facts of the allegation, conduct an initial risk assessment, and formulate a short-term risk management plan. (We discuss this process in Chapter 7.) As previously stated, a supervisor should be informed as well as a detective or specialist investigating officer. The victim should not be sent away on the basis that no crime has taken place and that this is not a law enforcement matter. We would suggest to the reader that the fact the individual has deemed it significant enough to report to law enforcement that she is being stalked suggests that she is at high risk of some form of honor-based violence.

Offenses Abroad

As we have already discussed, families are not averse to taking their children or family members abroad to commit HBV offenses. The reasons for this may include:

- The countries to which they travel are supportive of HBV practices in all its many facets.

- The punishment afforded suspects, if court is substantially reduced, than that from which the country they have travelled.
- They can exert more control over the individual.
- They can isolate the individual and, therefore, make her more vulnerable.
- They can more effectively hide their crime; this may be significant in the deposition of a body/bodies.

To obtain the relevant evidence or have access to suspects, witnesses, and/or victims will involve nation-to-nation support. Investigating officers should seek advice from their prosecuting agency and national government as to the best and most effective way of obtaining assistance from foreign countries. The stark reality is that, if governments are not on friendly terms, then it may well be impossible to obtain the relevant evidence, assist a vulnerable victim, and/or hold a perpetrator to account.

Conclusion

We have discussed in this chapter specific offense types that are common to HBV and issues that investigators need to consider. As we have seen, HBV presents particular challenges that need to be taken into consideration to achieve an effective investigation. In the next chapter, we move on to consider further issues within secondary investigation, exploring the role of particular specialists such as family liaison officers (FLOs), the role of senior managers within HBV investigations, and the prosecution of HBV offenders.

Effective Investigation of Honor-Based Violence Offenses 4

6

Secondary Investigation, Family Liaison Officers, Supervision, and Prosecution

In this chapter, we continue the discussion of the secondary investigation of honor-based violence (HBV) offenses by exploring the role of family liaison officers and senior managers in HBV investigations. We then will move on to discuss the prosecution of HBV offenses.

Family Liaison Officers (FLOs)

In an investigation of serious crime, there are situations in which it is advisable to deploy a family liaison officer (FLO). We recommend that in all HBV investigation, a FLO should be appointed. The FLO role is a specialist investigator role for which officers are specially selected and trained. In the United Kingdom and other jurisdictions, law enforcement uses FLOs as a means of interacting with families and victims, offering support and guidance, and providing advice and updates on the progress of the investigation to the police. FLOs also act as investigators within the family, collecting information and making observations in support of the investigation. FLOs are assigned to particular families or victims and remain assigned to them for as long as they are required in an investigation. As an investigating officer, the FLO works under the guidance of the lead investigator and will be tasked to ask specific questions or obtain certain information. Though a particular jurisdiction may not specifically use FLOs, it is possible for any officer, who has suitable skills and experience to perform this task.

If a FLO is assigned in an HBV investigation, it is best that he/she have knowledge and experience of HBV issues. It is important that FLOs must recognize that their primary responsibility is to the investigation and not to the family. It, therefore, is important that FLOs understand there may be certain information that they will not be able to give to the family and information that they may not be privy to so as not to compromise an investigation.

The FLO should be debriefed on a regular basis by the lead investigating officer and also should be afforded access to Occupational Health or other recognized support service. Given the complexities of an HBV deployment, FLOs can, if not adequately supported, be subject to significant stress and may become "burnt out" very quickly.

FLO Selection

HBV investigations can continue for many months, even years, so a FLO deployment can be a long and involved role. Therefore, we recommend that FLOs assigned a role in an HBV investigation should have a deputy, and they should have the time, capacity, and resilience to fulfill their role. It is important that, when considering the appointment of a FLO and his/her deputy, consideration is given to identifying the persons most suitable to work with the respective family or victim. There are many relevant variables, such as the individual's training, experience capacity, and capability, as well as their gender, cultural background, age, and knowledge of HBV.

FLO Strategy

When a FLO is deployed, there should be a specific FLO strategy in place so that the FLO is aware of his/her role, the needs of the lead investigator, and the needs of the investigation. The development of a FLO strategy is a dynamic process and must be reviewed on a regular basis between the FLO and lead investigator.

A FLO strategy should include the summary of events and circumstances leading up to the offense as known at that time. It should include an overall aim, e.g.:

> The primary aim of this strategy is to facilitate the police investigation into the circumstances of the death of (name of deceased), supporting the investigative aims and objectives while preventing harm to others within the family or associated with the family.

The main objectives of a FLO strategy should aim to:

- Identify those family members who require a FLO and organize their deployment. The dynamics of the family and the community need to be taken into consideration in all HBV deployments and should be done on a case by case basis.
- Secure the confidence and trust of victims, family members, partners, and community members thereby enhancing their contribution to the investigation.

- Gather evidence and information from the family in a manner that contributes to the investigation, identifies risk, and supports a successful judicial outcome.
- Inform and create a depiction of the victim(s) lifestyle, and background with the intention of identifying suspects, the reason for the death (if an honor killing or suicide), and identifying potential future victims.
- Provide practical support and appropriate information (as approved by the lead investigator) in a sensitive and compassionate manner to the family, maintaining an awareness of the general issues surrounding HBV enquiries. This may include signposting victim's or family members to appropriate HBV nongovernment organizations (NGOs) who will provide practical guidance and support.
- Provide appropriate information (as approved by the lead investigator) and to facilitate care, advice, and support of any family member who subsequently may become at risk of harm or otherwise require support as a result of a crime.
- Establish a safe, effective, and appropriate communication link between vulnerable family members and the lead investigating officer. This should define contact parameters, and these parameters should be documented and noted by the senior investigating officer (SIO). A FLO engaged in a covert relationship with a family member needs to be fully aware of the parameters of his/her relationship in respect of both the needs of the enquiry and the requirements of the jurisdiction he/she is working in. The mere fact that this relationship is in place may be considered sufficient by some family members to kill their relative.
- Carry out effective and ongoing family risk assessments, which need to be completed to enable risks to be identified, assessed, and managed effectively by the lead investigator or other investigative unit.
- Support family members through the criminal justice process or civil court process. Again this is most effectively achieved if NGO partner's skills are utilized.
- Provide an opportunity for family members to have a voice in investigation meetings so that the enquiry can, if deemed appropriate, meet their needs and requirements.

As with any strategy, the FLO strategy is dynamic and needs to be reviewed regularly as the investigation matures. This is especially important in the event of any significant development that may affect the FLO's relationship with the family, thereby requiring a change in tactics.

FLO Priority Actions

When a FLO is deployed in an HBV investigation, there are certain priority actions that a lead investigator may wish to consider. The following considerations are not exhaustive and should be adapted on a case by case basis:

- Conduct local intelligence checks with respect to the initial and separate risk assessments for deployment to meet the family.
- Facilitate the lead investigating officer meeting the family.
- Risk assess other family members as they may be at significant risk of harm. The use of appropriate risk assessment tools should be used to both identify and manage risk.
- Identify all family members and community members who may be involved or have an interest in the enquiry. This will include compiling a family tree showing the relationship between all persons and, if at all possible, the hierarchy of the family. This also will include details of families who may be in foreign countries and who still may be part of the family decision-making process.
- Where family counsels or meetings are held, FLOs should obtain as much detail as possible about these and who is involved in them.
- Identify barriers to communication, be they language, physical, or safety, and discuss viable safe communication links.
- Identify family members, family associates, relevant addresses (residential and work), phone numbers, work places, places frequented, premises family members have control of, vehicles used, social networking sites, etc.
- Identify family's country of origin including region, town/village, etc., because these details could be significant to the investigation, especially where forced marriage is an issue.
- Identify friends, acquaintances, and other members of the victim's community who the victim may have come into contact with and their relevance her. This will enable the lead investigator to assess their relevance to the enquiry and who to prioritize speaking to.
- Identify a list of both statutory and nonstatutory agencies the victim may have had contact with to enable research to be undertaken to capture all relevant information, intelligence, and evidence.
- Obtain victimology statements. These will detail a victim's lifestyle, personality characteristics, and may potentially identify motive, suspects, and risk. A caveat should be placed here that any information obtained from family, friends, and community should be considered in the light of its validity and accuracy given the desire of those supportive of HBV practices to derail any enquiry.

- Obtain antemortem data with respect to a deceased victim, either for postdeath identification or to hold on record in anticipation of the worst case scenario if the victim is later killed. Personal Descriptive Forms (PDF)* of the victim or of all those in danger should be considered.
- If appropriate and in liaison with the lead investigator, establish safety protocols, identify escape plans, discuss covert techniques for contacting police, and discuss short-term risk management.

Record Keeping

The deployment and work of a FLO in an HBV investigation can have a dramatic effect on an investigation. It is important, therefore, that any contact made with the family or family member is recorded by the FLO, and details of any conversation held and information obtained is recorded accurately. The information should be passed to the lead investigator and investigation team at the earliest opportunity after meeting or having contact with the family.

All meetings and notes should be recorded and retained for both evidential and legal disclosure purposes. Ideally, this will be undertaken in a specific FLO log that should be regularly supervised by the lead investigator or other senior-nominated person at designated intervals. This log should under no circumstances be taken to any family meetings lest it compromises the investigation and law enforcement family relationship.

Where sensitive information is provided to the FLO, an alternative log should be considered that contains sensitive information. Due to our desire not to reveal covert policing methods, we do not intend to discuss the specifics of when such books should be started and what information they should contain. The lead investigator should make a note in his decision logs as to why a sensitive FLO log is being used and the rationale behind a sensitive log.

Family Confidence

A FLO should never be used in any role that could undermine the family's confidence in him/her. As mentioned previously, care must be taken that a FLO does not stray into the area of forming covert relationships with family members as designated by statute, e.g., the family member becomes a Covert Human Information Source (informant) without the proper legal safeguards to protect the family member and the information the family member provides.

---

* PDFs are a means of recording individual's descriptions, such as gender, ethnicity, height, size, hair, etc. It can include any descriptive feature as considered appropriate by the lead investigator.

FLO Communication Policy

A clear and coherent FLO communication policy is needed as part of any FLO strategy including deciding which individuals within the family group with whom the FLO will make contact. The family may be split into separate factions and how the FLO strategy manages this may be of significance. The lead investigating officer should meet with the family together with the FLO as soon as practicable and in accordance with the family wishes. This establishes a personal link and ensures the needs of the family are met and expectations are managed. Contact with the family should only be undertaken under the direction of the lead investigating officer or nominated deputy. This is so the relationship between family and FLO can be effectively managed and supervised.

Family Expectations

Careful thought needs to be given to managing family expectations in HBV cases, particularly where there are suspects in the family who may be under investigation. Clarity needs to be given to the family about the role of the FLO, e.g., hours of duty, how they can contact the FLO, and what law enforcement can deliver. Families should be warned that the FLO deployment is likely to be lengthy, but, at some time in the future, the FLO will exit the family. The families should be reassured that this will be done in a managed and controlled way and may involve the engagement or continued engagement of partner agencies.

Where FLO engagements are lengthy, families should be made aware that as much as possible, the same FLO will remain engaged; however, given that officers may move on, leave the service, or have other commitments, new FLOs may be introduced to the family. If this is to be the case, this should be done in a managed and staged way so that the transition from one FLO to another is as seamless as possible.

Relationship Breakdown With FLOs

Where a relationship breaks down between the FLO and the family, the lead investigating officer should meet with the family to identify the pertinent issues and what can be done to resolve these issues. This may include changing the FLO or working through intermediaries, such as family solicitors or community groups.

FLOs and the Media

Some HBV investigations may attract a significant amount of press interest and, therefore, it may be incumbent on the FLO to work with law enforcement media officers and the family to deliver on the lead investigating officer media strategy. The FLO should (unless otherwise directed by the lead investigating officer) inform the family of all press releases and pass statements to the family prior to publication. The FLOs should *not* themselves issue statements to the media unless directed to do so and in consultation with a law enforcement media officer.

Threats

Where FLOs become aware of a threat or immediate risk to an individual, they should immediately inform the lead investigating officer so that risk management strategies can be implemented at the earliest opportunity. It is not the role of the FLO to make operational or tactical decisions. These should be made by the lead investigator or a senior risk manager. The FLO provides the information and intelligence for those decisions to be made around managing risk.

Timeline of Events

The FLO should, once he/she starts collecting information, consider developing a time line of events and significant dates; this task may be done in conjunction with a trained intelligence analyst who will have access to specific software to compile this information.

FLOs and the Arrest of Family Members

Where arrests of family members are to take place, deliberation should occur as to the FLO's involvement, especially where he/she has built up a significant relationship with the family, and when the arrest will include search and seizure of property. Any decision to include a FLO in an arrest operation should be documented by the lead investigating officer providing a rational for his/her use. Considerations should include:

- How a FLO's involvement will affect his/her relationship with the family and what is the best way to progress this in relation to the family.
- Would the presence of the FLO support or hinder events at this stage of the investigation?

Interview of Family Members

Consideration also should be given as to whether to involve the FLO in any interviews of family members. With respect to an interview, the lead investigator should consider

- Whether the FLO's knowledge of the circumstances of the case is such that it might inadvertently contaminate the interviewing process.
- Whether the FLO has the skills necessary to undertake such an interview.
- The extent to which the FLO's position within the family is likely to be compromised by the need to challenge a witness's or suspect's account.
- Whether it is realistic and reasonable to expect the FLO to remain sufficiently objective in view of the particular circumstances of the case.

FLOs and Court

An area of heightened risk and considerable FLO input will be at any court appearance, especially if members of the family are estranged, are prosecution witnesses, or are unfamiliar with that particular country's legal system. The FLO will work very closely with the family at these key times, especially during a trial. It is essential that the lead investigating officer is briefed daily as to the wants, needs, and requirements of the family so that where possible their expectations are met. It is advisable that NGOs and, if available, court services are used to support the family, thus ensuring the court experience is less stressful.

Exiting Families

An exit from a family where HBV is concerned can be a difficult and drawn out process. The FLO(s) should be given support and guidance from the lead investigating officer. The exit should take place when all the FLO strategy objectives have been met. The FLO should have already had a discussion with the family about an eventual exit and this should have been reinforced as well by the lead investigating officer when he met the family. The point of exit should never come as a surprise to the family nor should it be done where there is substantial ongoing risk to family members.

FLO Welfare

The welfare of the FLOs should be monitored throughout their deployment and, if necessary, appropriate professional support should be utilized. At the conclusion of their FLO deployment, they should be fully debriefed by the lead investigator and offered occupational support and guidance services because this type of deployment can affect an officer's well being. In addition, by having a structured debrief organizational, learning can be captured so that future deployments may be enhanced and a better service delivered.

Having considered the role of FLOs, we now move on to consider the role of supervisors in the management of HBV investigations.

Supervision of Investigations

As with any major investigation, adequate supervision of investigators is important. This helps to ensure that an investigation progresses in an efficient manner. It is important that, at all stages of an investigation, investigating officers should not work in isolation, but should be subject to supportive supervision. In this section, we consider important tasks for supervisors in HBV investigations.

Investigation Review

Given the complexity of HBV investigations, we recommend that investigation supervisors carry out regular proactive reviews of investigations. These reviews should aim to ensure investigating officers are undertaking a professionally competent investigation in a timely manner, identifying all lines of enquiry, ensuring evidence is being gathered in an appropriate and systematic manner, that sufficient risk management plans are in place, and, if necessary, liaison with key partner agencies has taken place.

In undertaking regular reviews, supervisors will be in a better position to identify where there is a need for further resources, that the investigation is being undertaken in a professional manner in line with standard police procedures, and all potential lines of enquiry are explored.

Review of Primary Investigation

The first review should follow the completion of the primary investigation and preempt the start of the secondary investigation. The primary investigation and the associated allegation(s) need to be reviewed by a supervisory officer so that

- Any shortcomings in the primary investigation are identified and rectified at the earliest opportunity given the significant risk associated with HBV crimes.
- The secondary investigation is conducted by the most suitable law enforcement unit.

Timing of Reviews

We suggest that in the early stages of an investigation, reviews should occur every 24 hours. Depending on the seriousness of the investigation and the level of risk faced by an individual, the reviews can then be moved to every

48 hours, 72 hours, weekly, or monthly. The review process should be part of a broader investigative management strategy and be geared to ensuring the law enforcement response meets the need of the victim, the family, and community while upholding the reputation of the organization.

Assigning Secondary Investigators

One of the roles of the supervisor, following the review of the primary investigation, will be to assign the secondary investigation to appropriate investigators. The secondary investigation should be assigned to an individual officer or team with the most appropriate skills and capacity to undertake a thorough and comprehensive investigation. When the secondary investigation is assigned, the supervisory officer should produce a written investigative plan highlighting aims and objectives of the investigation, immediate actions, and investigative priorities. This is to ensure risk is effectively managed, the investigation has direction, and the aims of the investigation are clear to all investigators.

Depending on local practices, honor killings could be investigated by specialist homicide investigation teams. Though these teams will have specific expertise and experience in the investigation of homicide, they may not have any or have very limited knowledge of honor killings and HBV. We advise, if this is the case, that an officer with substantial knowledge of HBV be attached to the team to inform the lead investigating officer and the investigation team of issues they may encounter.

As already mentioned, supervisors at this stage should build in reviews to ensure work is being completed in a timely and satisfactory manner, as well as identifying the need for additional support or identifying further lines of enquiry. It should be noted that this "third eye" provided by reviews may prove invaluable particularly as some HBV investigations are complex and it is possible for investigators to get lost under a mountain of information and actions they need to undertake.

Ad Hoc Supervision and Review

While setting a timetable for reviews, it is also important for supervisors to be willing to carry out ad hoc supervision and reviews of investigations. This is because many HBV investigations can change direction rapidly as information comes in to the enquiry. In these circumstances, there can be a need for a significant change in the direction of the investigation.

Documentation

All supervisory actions and reviews should be recorded in a retrievable format so that these can be seen by the assigned investigators and they are aware of the direction of the investigation and the needs and requirements of their management.

Responsibilities

It is important that supervisors ensure that all secondary investigative officers are aware of their role, the requirements of their supervisors in line with the current investigative plan, and the overall status of the investigation. How this is done will be dictated by how individual police units manage their crime investigations.

Following the identification, arrest, and charging of suspects in HBV cases, a prosecution may take place. In the next section, we consider some of the important issues in the prosecution of those charges with HBV offenses.

Prosecution of HBV Offenses

We have already discussed the difficulties law enforcement may have in investigating HBV allegations, and the challenges faced by prosecution lawyers can be equally complex and challenging. Therefore, it is important that any prosecuting lawyer who progresses an HBV case has an understanding of and experience in working with HBV. The reason for this is that a robust and professional case can be presented to the court, victims and those associated with them feel confident in the legal system, communities feel confident that prosecutors understand HBV cases, and it allows the best opportunity to hold the perpetrator to account, reinforcing the message that HBV will not be tolerated.

Complexity of HBV

As we have discussed, many HBV offenses are very complex. For example, in the United Kingdom, the Crown Prosecution Service (CPS), the criminal prosecution agency, conducted a study of the prosecution of forced marriage and HBV crimes (CPS, 2008). The research indicated that prosecutions regularly involved more than one defendant, and in nearly 50% of cases identified offenses were committed against more than one individual. As regards honor killing, the findings indicated that there were often at least three people involved in the encouragement, planning, commission, and attempts to cover up the murder. It also is regularly the case that not all of those responsible are within the jurisdiction of the prosecuting agency. Given this, it can be argued that some cases of HBV may be considered analogous to organized criminality and prosecutors may note that the tools used to prosecute organized criminal networks may be of benefit to successfully prosecute HBV cases.

Early Consultation

Given the complexity of HBV, it is essential that when law enforcement begins investigating an HBV offense with a view to prosecuting in a criminal court, early consultation should take place between prosecutor and police. This is to ensure that all potential evidence can be identified and the best use of that evidence can be discussed. The partnership between law enforcement and prosecuting agencies should continue throughout the investigation and should include all prosecuting barristers/attorneys.

Covert Strategies

Given that some families may utilize contract killers or other professional criminals to carry out the offenses, in HBV investigations there is at times a need to utilize covert investigative strategies. In these circumstances, it is important to carefully balance the needs of the investigation to secure evidence that can be presented to a court against protecting the victim and witnesses. As always, the safety of the victim and witnesses should be paramount. Where such covert intelligence techniques are used, there always should be discussion between law enforcement and prosecutors to ensure that any evidence gathered and the techniques used will stand up to scrutiny in a criminal court.

Risk to Victims

Prosecutors need to be aware of the risk faced by victims and witnesses and the relationships between them and suspects (they are often relatives) in HBV cases. These factors may often lead to victims being very mistrusting of the legal system and reluctant to engage with it. It is important then that both law enforcement and prosecutors are fully versed in the relevant legislation and policies in relation to victim and witness care. Victim and witness care is a key consideration in any prosecution strategy to ensure the witnesses stay engaged and supportive of any prosecution.

Decisions to Prosecute

Prosecutors should always consider cases pragmatically regardless of how sensitive a case may be. There must be sufficient evidence to provide a realistic opportunity of prosecution. This is to ensure that HBV victims and those supporting the victims remain engaged with criminal prosecuting agencies, they have confidence in the system, and vast amounts of public resources are not wasted on weak cases with little chance of success. Where cases are not prosecuted, we recommend that prosecutors and police meet with the victim and others, such as relevant NGOs, to explain the rationale behind decisions and to highlight the vulnerabilities of the case.

Disclosure of Evidence to Defense

Depending upon the jurisdiction, the issue of disclosure to defense teams can be a significant consideration for prosecutors, notably where covert methods have been used to secure evidence or where mutual aid has been obtained from an international police force. Key considerations for a prosecutor are whether disclosure of information places someone in danger, whether covert law enforcement tactics are revealed, or whether the information is relevant to prosecuting the case in question. Every case will have to be looked at individually and, where information is not disclosed, a sound and robust rationale should be recorded.

In terms of who should decide on disclosure issues, we recommend as a general rule of thumb that the greater the perceived risk to an individual, or the law enforcement organization, the more senior the decision maker should be. It may ultimately fall to a trial judge to decide what can and will be disclosed. Where judicial decisions require disclosure of material to a defense team, we recommend that law enforcement and prosecutors consider the advisability of disclosure, being mindful of the risk to victims, witnesses, and law enforcement strategies balanced against the public interest of continuing with the trial. Prosecutors also should be mindful that disclosure rules in a criminal court may differ significantly from disclosure rules in a civil or family court.

Prosecution of Minors

An issue for police and prosecutors is the use of children/minors to commit HBV offenses. As we have noted, families may use the younger members of families to deflect the attention of authorities away from those who have conspired to commit the criminal act by identifying them as the offender. In contrast, some families may even encourage involvement in HBV by minors, seeing it as a rite of passage into manhood. Whatever the reason families have for involving minors, this raises the issue of prosecuting children/minors for criminal offenses. Broadly, the issue of prosecuting minors needs to be considered with reference to local prosecution practices.

An additional issue in HBV cases involving minors is that there may be a need for prosecutors to prove a suspect's age. This most often occurs because it is important to explore if a child is within the age of criminal responsibility, as where a suspect claims to be a child, it may be an attempt to lessen the sentencing burden or facilitate a more favorable trial. In order to facilitate this prosecution, agencies need to consider:

- Liaising with other agencies to identify who the individual is, their age, and background, e.g., education, health, social services, etc.
- If the suspect is a migrant to the country and his identity is in question, there will be a need to undertake a variety of enquiries that may include asking for mutual assistance from another national jurisdiction to achieve identification.

Witness Protection During the Trial Process

Given the vulnerability of victims and some witnesses, certain protection measures may need to be put in place to enable them to present their evidence to court. These measures and the availability of the measures will vary by legal jurisdiction. Depending on the protective measures applicable to a jurisdiction, the following may apply and be worth consideration to facilitate witness protection:

- Witness anonymity.
- Voice distortion.
- Support from witness support services within either the court or other victims' charitable organizations.
- Involvement of HBV specialist agencies.
- Taking of victim's personal statements that will highlight to the court the effect the criminality being tried has had on them.
- Pretrial court visits to familiarize the witnesses with the court building, court room, and to effectively manage the witness expectations.
- Support in travelling to and from court as well as assistance with childcare when attending court.
- Ongoing risk management meetings/child strategy meetings to ensure the ongoing safety of the victim. It should be noted that these processes should not stop at the conclusion of any trial. As previously discussed, this should only cease when the risk no longer exists or where there is no more meaningful intervention required. The prosecutor should always be part of any risk management plan.
- Consultation with family and other community support networks that are known not to be supportive of HBV.

It is important to note that giving evidence in court may place some witnesses in danger for the rest of their lives and, therefore, protection measures may need to be in place for a considerable length of time regardless of whether the perpetrators are convicted and sentenced.

Child Witnesses

As with all childcare matters, the welfare of a child is paramount, as is the impact of the trial and his/her involvement in it upon his/her ongoing development. With respect to child victims and witnesses, consideration should not only be given to the child, but also to other family members supporting the child. Consent may be needed for the child to give evidence, and care should be taken in what the prosecution discloses to individuals to obtain that consent so that it doesn't impact on the fairness of a trial.

Vulnerable Adults

As we also have discussed earlier in this book, adults who are either physically disabled or have support needs due to mental capacity are vulnerable to HBV, most notably forced marriage. It is important that where these victims of HBV are identified, both law enforcement and prosecutors have in place adequate and appropriate support mechanisms to ensure the evidence they provide is both admissible and that they can provide the best possible evidence. Thus, consideration should be given to using specialist HBV NGOs to support these witnesses and also to utilizing the resources of statutory and charitable organizations that can work with vulnerable adults. These organizations are likely to have the necessary specialist knowledge and skills to facilitate the relevant support for these individuals at a later date.

Use of Expert Evidence

Within jurisdictions that allow the use of expert witnesses, prosecution can be supported by the provision of "expert evidence" from individuals who not only have an understanding of HBV, but also about HBV within affected communities. Expert evidence of this sort may greatly assist the court in its deliberations, providing contextual information that aids understanding of the issues.

There are many areas in which expert witness testimony may prove useful, including:

- Ensuring the court has an understanding of the subject matter.
- Rebuttal of evidence put forward by defendants as they try to justify a criminal offense as a "cultural" or "religious" issue, as is often the case.
- Explaining the reticence and reluctance of a witness to provide evidence in open court.
- Highlighting to the court the significant risk that witnesses may place themselves in by giving evidence and the ongoing effect this will have on their lives post trial.

However, with all expert witnesses come caveats, and it should not be assumed that if a witness is an expert in HBV issues he/she will be equally adept at dealing with wider cultural, geographical, or religious issues. Therefore, the use of expert witnesses should always be considered in not only what they may add to a prosecution case, but also what negative effect they may have on the case if their testimony is undermined. It is important then that, for witnesses used in this capacity, the relevant prosecuting agency knows not only what their area of expertise is, but also what the limit of their knowledge is. The use of NGOs should be considered a useful tool in identifying good, knowledgeable, expert witnesses, as well as using specialists in statutory agencies and not withstanding specialist police investigators.

Use of Interpreters

When using interpreters and translators, prosecutors should be aware that, if the individual is not an approved law enforcement translator, there is potential that the individual may be part of the family, community, or linked groups who could be sympathetic to HBV. As language barriers can be a key area of isolation for the victim, it is important that any individual used in this capacity is approved, independent, and professional so that the integrity of the translation can be assured.

Immigration Status

Another area where prosecutors should be mindful when considering barriers to a successful prosecution is the immigration status of a victim or a witness. This may limit the witness's ability to access public funds and support from NGOs. There also may be a reluctance to come forward for fear of deportation, which may increase the risk to the witness's well being. When the victim has an insecure immigration status, then specialist advice should be sought in an attempt to resolve pertinent issues in an appropriate and timely fashion. This may include seeking advice from statutory agencies, NGOs, or lawyers with an expertise in immigration matters. We have already discussed the international dimension of HBV; therefore, where law enforcement engages in early consultation with prosecutors, this will assist in areas such as extradition and mutual requests for assistance from other states. This early consultation will prevent cases being impeded at a later date.

Conclusion

In this chapter, we have considered the use of specialists, such as FLOs, to aid in an investigation. We have highlighted the importance of effective supervision in investigating complex crimes, such as HBV, and considered the prosecution of HBV.

Ultimately, because of the complex and diverse nature of HBV crimes, it is important that the law enforcement and prosecutors work together to maximize both the quantity and quality of evidence that is presented to the court. It is important that both law enforcement investigating and the lawyers prosecuting have an understanding of HBV so that the strongest possible case can be built. The risk of harm to individuals is high and the risk of losing community confidence is also high if both police and prosecutors fail to discharge their duties to the highest professional standards.

Over the previous four chapters, we have explored the investigation and prosecution of HBV offenses. We have considered the role of the primary and secondary investigating officer, the challenges presented by various types of HBV offense, and the role of specialists, such as FLOs and supervisors. We are hopeful that we have convinced the reader that to undertake an effective investigation will require knowledge, appropriate skills, and experience of HBV; without this, such are the complexities of HBV investigations where there is a considerable risk that law enforcement may inadvertently expose victims to significant risk, fail to identify evidential opportunities, and, therefore, lose the confidence of victims, family members, and communities alike.

We have noted in the previous chapters that victims and witnesses in HBV face considerable risks and the importance for investigators to carry out timely and regular risk assessment and develop strategies to manage the associated risk. In the next chapter, we move on to consider risk management in the context of HBV.

Risk Management Victim Risk and Community Impact Assessment

7

The risks facing victims and some witnesses of honor-based violence (HBV) should not be underestimated and, as stated in previous chapters, this can include a significant risk of serious physical assault and even homicide. Adequate risk assessment and management, therefore, is crucial when investigating HBV-related offenses in order to prevent this. Indeed, it is perhaps not overstating the issue to suggest that, because of the high risk of death facing victims of HBV, any law enforcement investigation or enquiry by another agency into an honor-based violence matter should be seen as *homicide prevention*.

In a similar vein, HBV crimes can have a negative impact upon both the affected and broader community with the potential for violence or other outcomes that significantly impact upon community cohesion. Law enforcement, therefore, needs to consider not only the risk to victims but also the impact of HBV upon communities.

It is the purpose of this chapter to explore the issue of risk management within HBV investigations. We will define what we mean by risk management before moving on to explore specific strategies and risk management methods that have demonstrated utility within an HBV context. We will begin by considering risk as it concerns victims of HBV before ending the chapter with a consideration of the assessment of the impact of HBV on communities.

What Is Risk Management?

Risk management can be defined as a process involving the identification, assessment, and prioritization of threats of harm to an individual or individuals followed by the coordinated and economical application of resources to minimize, monitor, and control the likelihood of harm. While this definition encapsulates the basic idea of risk management, it does beg the question of what we mean by *risk, harm, risk identification,* and *risk assessment.* Below, we briefly introduce these concepts before moving on to discuss risk management in the context of HBV.

Defining Terms

In the context of risk management, *risk* is associated with *harm* and the likelihood of the harm occurring. *Harm,* when referring to crime and criminality, generally refers to damage to the well being of individuals and includes some combination of physical, sexual, or psychological damage. *Risk identification* refers to the identification of particular types of harm, and *risk assessment* refers to the active consideration of factors related to a particular type of harm and the likelihood of its occurrence. *Risk management,* therefore, can be considered to be concerned with the strategy or strategies used to militate against various forms of harm.

In general, risk identification, risk assessment, and risk management are related because, when a form of harm is identified and assessed to be likely, there is often strong motivation to reduce the risk of harm, and this requires risk management. For example, the identification of a given hazard, such as the threat of homicide for an HBV victim, as having a high risk of occurring is of interest, but does not help protect against the harm. Risk management would be an attempt to reduce the risk of harm.

Risk Identification

The first step in any risk management process is the identification of particular risks or hazards that may lead to harm. In the context of violence risk management, the *hazard* is usually the behavior of another person that is likely to cause harm, e.g., some form of violent attack. It is important to clearly and unambiguously identify the hazard, however, so that it is clear what has been risk assessed. For example, in the case of HBV, the hazard could be "a violent attack by a family member." This may seem straightforward, but we need to be clear what is, and is not, "violence." Is verbal violence included in our definition or only acts that result in physical harm? If we define violence in terms of physical harm, do we then need to specify what degree of harm we mean? Does this include harm on a spectrum from cuts and bruises through to death, or only fatal violence? It is important to note that, in the absence of clearly specified hazards, the results of a risk assessment can be ambiguous and, ultimately, useless. If we do not define clearly our terms of reference, including in our example above, the scale of the violence, the target of the violence, and the level of injury caused by the violence, the user of a risk assessment will be left uncertain as to what exactly we are referring to.

Risk Factors

Within any risk assessment there are *risk factors* that serve to increase or decrease the risk of a hazard occurring. For each different hazard, there are likely to be a number of shared and specific risk factors that may raise or lower the risk of the hazard. Those assessing risk, therefore, need to be cognizant that the same risk factors may have very different relationships to different hazards. Hence, even if some risk factors are related to the risk of a homicidal attack, they may not necessarily be related to other forms of HBV, such as female genital mutilation.

Dynamic and Static Risk Factors

There are two classes of risk factors: *dynamic* and *static*. Static risk factors are factors that do not change over time. In general, these are historical or categorical factors that cannot be modified. Examples of *static risk factors* include gender, nationality, date of birth, features of an individual's upbringing, and past experiences. *Dynamic risk factors* do change over time and can be either under or out of the control of individuals. For example, dynamic factors within the control of individuals might be arranging family meetings and actively encouraging others to attack a victim. Dynamic factors out of an individual's control might include the availability of weapons, attitudes of other family members to HBV, or the activities of law enforcement. It is likely that any hazard will be associated with both dynamic and static risk factors. Frequently, an error made in risk assessment and management is an exclusive focus on historical or static risk factors that can produce highly misleading assessments. Risk assessment also should include dynamic risk factors, although this has implications for how often a risk assessment should be done, as we discuss below.

Repeated Risk Assessment

The risk of any hazard changes over time, due in large part to the aforementioned dynamic risk factors. For example, law enforcement activity may make preparatory acts for an HBV-related crime harder to carry out, which may reduce the risk for violence they pose. Similarly, risk of violence may be increased with the arrival of other members of a family who are supportive of HBV. The hazard also may change over time with the arrival of some members of a family perhaps changing the dynamics and activities of the family group, possibly developing a focus upon another form of HBV. Those doing risk assessment need to be aware then of the changing situation, and make statements about the *current* level of risk, assuming various contingencies. For example, a risk assessment may consider the risk assuming there is no intervention by law enforcement or social services, the possible changes in risk following a specified intervention, the risk assuming no change in family group composition, or even the risk assuming specified changes.

Risk assessments should be carried out on a regular basis to reflect such possible changes. A difficulty lies, however, in identifying when to carry out each risk assessment. Should this be daily, weekly, monthly? The regularity of a risk assessment should be determined by the particular circumstances. For example, the level of risk may change suddenly should changes occur within a family's structure, such as if a daughter runs away from the family home, as we have noted that, in the case of HBV, the risk of a violent assault is significantly increased in these circumstances should the family gain access to the daughter. More regular risk assessments should be made, then, for situations such as these as compared with situations in which there are no changes in circumstances. Essentially, risk assessment should be flexible and related to the demands of the particular circumstances.

Relative Risk

For any hazard, some risk factors will raise and others will reduce the likelihood of the hazard causing harm. Risk assessment, therefore, needs to be sensitive to both drivers and inhibitors of risk. One of the difficulties when carrying out risk assessment is that assessors can pay insufficient attention to factors that reduce a risk. These risk factors can be just as important as factors that increase the risk of a hazard. Essentially, for a risk assessment to be useful, it should specify the conditions in which the risk of harm will be raised or reduced over a specified time. For example, an individual reporting her fear of HBV to law enforcement may increase the risk she faces, whereas risk may be reduced should an individual be able to move to a new area. The judgment for the risk assessment becomes how to balance different effects of different risk factors.

In the context of HBV, the risk management strategies employed may themselves be regarded as dynamic risk factors that should be incorporated into future risk assessments. This is because these are likely to influence the opportunity an individual has to engage in behavior relevant to the hazard.

Risk Management and HBV

In HBV cases, risk can manifest itself in many different ways including deliberate physical or sexual assault, kidnapping, mental torture, or the threat of carrying out such an act. Given the possibility of such serious violence, we suggest that, in all cases where HBV is suspected, risk management practices should be proactive, not reactive. A useful initial assumption for the investigator charged with carrying out the initial risk assessment is that the victim may be at a significant risk of harm. In this context, it is important to note that every victim has a fundamental right to be believed and should never be turned away by any law enforcement officer, airport official, customs officer, or from a police station, housing, or social work department, or other place managed by statutory authorities. The case detailed below is a salutary reminder of the potential impact of disbelieving or turning away a victim of HBV.

> Razan Fayez was working as a family law attorney at the Tahirih Justice Center, a Virginia-based nonprofit organization that helps women and children around the world who are fleeing forced marriages, so-called "honor violence," and genital mutilation in places like Togo and Pakistan find safety in the United States. However, things changed one Wednesday morning when Fayez got a call from an attorney working with a women's shelter in Texas. The shelter, said the caller, needed advice on how to help a 16-year-old girl who had run away from home because her parents were about to send her overseas to enter a forced marriage. Now, said the caller, the parents were threatening to sue the shelter if they kept the girl. "I remember feeling an overwhelming sense of urgency," says Fayez. "If she goes off to be married against her will, she'll be raped." Fayez advised that the shelter could go to court and file an order of protection for the girl against her parents. She scrambled to make connections; child protective services apparently said they didn't want to get involved in a "cultural issue," remembers Fayez, but it was for naught. When she came to work the next Monday, the attorney for the shelter said the girl had gone back to her family.

Information Sharing

In order to make effective risk management decisions, the investigator needs to be in possession of the best and most detailed information. In this regard, it is essential that agencies have information-sharing agreements between themselves so that information can be collated to fully understand the circumstances and all the parties involved.

Cultural Background

As part of a risk assessment, it is important for investigators to consider the cultural background of a victim's family. As we have mentioned in previous chapters, once a victim contacts an agency and reveals her concerns and seeks help, the risks to her will escalate. In these circumstances, the victim may be viewed as bringing unwanted attention from the authorities onto the family and be seen as a traitor to the immediate and/or extended family and community. This reaction, in part, often stems from the experiences of family members with law enforcement and the tools of the state. Many of the victim's immediate and extended family members may come from countries where law enforcement agencies and the instruments of state are not trusted, may be corrupt, or have exercised excessive power and control over citizens or specific sections of the community. This engenders fear and distrust of authorities that is likely to compound feelings and attitudes that support honor-based violence leading to a strong conviction that the victim needs to be punished and may form a powerful justification (in the eyes of perpetrators) for violence.

Models of Risk Identification and Assessment in HBV

There are a number of different models to identify and assess risk in suspected HBV. Notable among them is the United Kingdom's Association of Chief Police Officers (ACPO) Domestic Abuse, Stalking, Harassment, and Honor-Based Violence (DASH, 2009).[*] The DASH tool, along with instructions for its use, can be found online at: http://www.dashriskchecklist.co.uk/uploads/pdfs/DASH%202009.pdf

The authors were actively involved in the design and implementation of the DASH tool throughout the United Kingdom and recommend its use as an example of best risk management practices. DASH is a simple-to-use risk assessment tool that requires the assessor, on the basis of information from the victim and other material from an investigation, to identify the presence or absence of particular risk factors and comment upon them across a range of domains related to the abuser's characteristics, the current situation, the history of violence, and the victim's experiences. As regards HBV, it contains items that are known risk factors for violence, for example:[†]

- Truanting: If the victim is less than 18 years old, is the victim truanting?
- Self-harm: Is there evidence of self-harm?
- House arrest and being "policed at home:" Is the victim being kept at home or her behavior activity being policed (describe the behaviors)?
- Fear of being forced into an engagement/marriage: Is the victim worried that she will be forced to marry against her will?
- Pressure to go abroad: Is the victim fearful of being taken abroad?

On completion of the DASH form and on the basis of presence of the risk factors identified and the assessor, one should make a decision concerning the level of risk faced by the victim.

---

[*] The Association of Chief Police Officers (ACPO, official title The Association of Chief Police Officers of England, Wales, and Northern Ireland), established in 1948, is a private limited company that leads the development of policing practice in England, Wales, and Northern Ireland. ACPO includes officers of the rank of assistance chief constable (in London this is the equivalent to commander) and above.

[†] Note that the items in the list are a selection of items from the DASH and not the complete list. Assessors would need to complete the entire risk tool to obtain an assessment of the risk.

Risk Assessment Levels

To inform risk management processes, risk assessments typically classify risk into a number of levels to indicate the degree of risk faced by a victim or victims. In the United Kingdom, law enforcement uses three risk levels: *Standard, Medium,* and *High Risk.* It is worthy of note that *standard risk* has replaced *low risk* as a risk level because the low level categorization can be perceived by some individuals as reason not to take any action in response to the risk. In specifying risk levels, it is important to define clearly what characterizes each level of risk. The aforementioned DASH model utilizes these risk levels and defines them as follows:

> **Standard** Risk: Current evidence does not indicate the likelihood of serious harm.
> **Medium** Risk: There are identifiable indicators of the risk of serious harm. The offender has the potential to cause serious harm, but is unlikely to do so unless there is a change in circumstances, e.g., failure to take medication, loss of accommodation, relationships breakdown, and drug or alcohol misuse.
> **High** Risk: There is identifiable indicators of the risk of serious harm. The potential could happen at any time and the impact would be serious.

It is important to note that the risk of serious harm is defined as:

> A risk that is life threatening and/or traumatic, and from which recovery, whether physical or psychological, can be expected to be difficult or impossible (OASys, U.K. Home Office, 2002*).

Utilizing a risk tool such as DASH has a number of distinct advantages over using nonsystematic risk assessments or even guess work. Decisions made using risk tools are less prone to personal bias than using nonsystematic approaches. This is because risk tools encourage investigators to systematically consider a wide range of evidence and information that they have available rather than focusing on information that an investigator might idiosyncratically regard as important. Systematic risk tools also tend to produce more reliable risk decisions—different investigators are more likely to agree with the risk level identified—because of the structured assessment of information. Essentially, each investigator is directed to consider the same information and make his decision following a similar process. Because DASH was developed through empirical research that has identified factors that are

---

* OASys is the abbreviated term for the Offender Assessment System, used in England and Wales by Her Majesty's Prison Service and the National Probation Service to measure the risks and needs of criminal offenders under their supervision.

associated with risk, decisions made using it are generally more defensible than if decisions are made in a more ad hoc manner because DASH decisions are evidence-based.

Risk tools, such as DASH, also allow the investigator to identify types of information that are related to risk of harm, but are presently unknown, thus contributing to the information collection prioritization effects of investigators. It is important to reiterate that risk levels can change over time and, thus, the investigator should be sensitive to this and be ready to change the assessment of risk should circumstances change.

Risk Assessment to Risk Management

After identifying and assessing the level of risk, the investigator then must consider a proportionate and effective plan to manage the identified risk(s). In addition, given the psychological impact on victims, it also is necessary to consider a plan to manage the victim's perception of risk.

In essence, a risk management plan does not need to be complicated as it needs to be clearly understood by those who will be leading and/or contributing to its delivery. A basic risk management model known as RARA (remove, avoid, reduce, accept) has been successfully practiced by the London Metropolitan Police Service (MPS).

RARA describes four important steps that are needed in any risk management plan. These include:

1. **Remove:** Measures should be considered that will serve to remove the risks faced by a victim. This might include approaches such as surveillance, carrying out an operation against the suspect(s), timely arrest of perpetrators for offenses either directly linked to the honor-based violence crime or incident under investigation, or for unrelated offenses if relevant, such as fraud or drug trafficking crimes, in order to remove them from the environment and thus posing a threat to the victim. Depending on the jurisdiction and rules of arrest that pertain, disruption of the activities of suspects may be considered, such as a repetitive program of disruptive arrests of people connected to the principal suspects or those orchestrating or otherwise conspiring to commit offenses against the victim. It is important that in attempts to remove the risk, investigators uphold ethical investigative principles and make every effort to gather quality evidence that will enable suspects to be remanded into custody should that be possible.

2. **Avoid:** This approach to risk management involves creating circumstances that allow the victim to avoid the risks faced. This could be achieved by placing the victim into a witness protection program

or relocating her to a secure address not known to the suspect(s) or indeed anyone else. The locations selected and the implementation of such a strategy must be given careful consideration in terms of how many and which individuals are aware of a victim's location. This is because it is not unusual for those with (or suspected to have) knowledge of a victim's whereabouts to be subject to surveillance by family, community members, or those employed by them, e.g., bounty hunters, or even to be threatened with violence in order to identify the location.

3. **Reduce:** This involves reduction of the risk faced by victims. This can be achieved by conducting disruption arrests and/or enforcement of the suspect's police- or court-imposed bail conditions, safety planning, or target hardening of addresses where the victim is.

4. **Accept:** There may be cases where investigators need to accept the risks against a victim. This is most likely under circumstances where the risk to a victim is thought to be at the low (standard) level. There, however, must be a constant reassessment of the information in such cases so that the risk levels can be constantly kept under review.

Table 7.1 provides examples of the kind of responses that can be made to various risk levels. As can be seen, as the risk level increases, so does the degree of intervention by law enforcement and other authorities to protect the victim.

In risk management, it is essential that investigators continue to collect relevant information and continue to review the level of risk. Collection of information allows judgments to be made about the utility of the risk management process and aids in decision making about when it should be reviewed. The lead investigator also must set review time limits for the reassessment of the risk and the accompanying risk management control plan.

The risk management plan should guide all of the actions. Risk assessment and risk management is not simply a "tick box" administrative process, it is a fundamental part of keeping the victim and others safe.

Risk Aversion Is No Decision

Risk averse decision making is when investigators fail to fully assess the risk and tend to rate it as *high*. It is important to note that while investigators may feel that this protects the victim (and, indeed, themselves) from the adverse consequences of judging a lower level of risk, such a strategy is counterproductive. It is likely to result in a failure to implement the appropriate risk management and to adequately manage the risk level, resulting in loss of resources for law enforcement and others. In addition, affecting arrests and

Table 7.1   Risk Management Mitigating Control Measures

Standard Risk	Medium Risk	High or Very High Risk
Provide victim with documented crime prevention and personal safety advice.	As standard risk plus …	As medium risk plus …
Signpost the victim to statutory and not-for-profit organizations that specialize in honor-based violence, Violence Against Women & Girls, etc.	Victim's address flagged on law enforcement computers (unless witness protection) to provide heightened response if called there	Place victim into the witness protection scheme; change identification, secret address, etc. If not a witness protection scheme, place at another safe house not known to family or community members
Advise her/him in use of the police emergency number	Allied to the above put in place a response plan, which must be activated if there's an emergency call to the address.	
	Trigger plan with action to be developed to support above	Surveillance operation using covert surveillance techniques (people and technology assets); gather intelligence and/or evidence to disrupt
Victim carries a cell phone	Install a cover trigger/panic alarm	If a child victim, then invoke child protection legislation, e.g., using legislation, remove child to a place of safety
Advise regarding court civil injunctions, e.g., forced marriage civil protection order, prevention of harassment order, or similar	Develop escape plan. Passport, birth certificate, bank cards, money, and clothing to be kept at a safe locations	Disruption arrests whether or not directly connected to the honor-based violence crimes
Law enforcement officers take the victim's photograph, DNA, and fingerprints with consent (to aid identification) if she/he goes missing	Provide a cell phone for covert use	Support the victim to obtain court orders, e.g., forced marriage civil protection order, prevention of harassment order, or similar
	Allocate officer as single point of contact (SPOC)	Direct approach and conduct meeting with the family; may act as a deterrent

(Continued)

Table 7.1   Risk Management Mitigating Control Measures (Continued)

Standard Risk	Medium Risk	High or Very High Risk
Consider placing a marker against the victim's name on law enforcement agencies computer systems (this will increase an officer's alert status should the officer find a victim in circumstances that heightens suspicions that the victim is at risk and generate a more in-depth investigation)	Discuss a danger signal in residence window (visible from public place)	Signpost victim to support/get trusted not-for-profit case worker to meet victim at a secure location (not witness protection address) for confidence building and moral support
	Surveillance of suspect(s) Disruption arrests of suspect(s)	With or without victim's consent, confidentially brief social workers, employers, school/colleague staff who can "look out" for the victim
	Visible police vehicle and foot patrol (by neighborhood officers)	
	Multiagency risk assessment (case) conference	

carrying out other actions that are disruptive of suspects (activity that is one response to a *high risk level* assessment) is likely to engender significant community disharmony, especially if the true risk to the victim was low. There is also the likelihood of negative victim reactions if her risk is erroneously rated as high. Risk assessment, therefore, must be realistic, and judgments should be made based on the information available only at the time of the assessment.

Should the victim and suspects of an HBV case be from a minority group, some investigators may feel less empowered to act for fear of being accused of racism. However, investigators should feel free to investigate all allegations of HBV. Cultural sensitivity, awareness, mutual understanding, and trust are fundamental in the delivery of services to the public. However, such sensitivity and awareness is not a reason *not* to act. Indeed, as former U.K. Government Minister Mike O'Brien stated, "Cultural sensitivity is no excuse for moral blindness."

Community Impact Assessment

When an honor crime (in particular, a homicide or other serious offense) takes place, often strong reactions to it are felt within the affected community, which also may have effects at a national and even international level. Reactions of shock, fear, and even denial of the occurrence of the crime are common. Often communities feel impelled to defend themselves by denying that the crime has an honor-based element and/or denying that HBV exists within the community.

HBV crimes may have a significant negative impact upon communities and community relations, increasing community fear and the risk of violence against community members and within communities. Given this, how are authorities to work to minimize the community impact of HBV? This brings us to another aspect of risk management, a consideration of the impact upon a community of an honor crime and an assessment of the risks of negative outcomes the crime itself or the attendant law enforcement activity might have.

Assessing the Impact of HBV on Communities

The risks to a community of HBV emphasize the need to ensure that a *Community Impact Assessment* is conducted. Essentially, this is a form of risk assessment, which analyzes HBV incidents and assesses their impact on either the whole community or a specific section of it. Once the community impact assessment is carried out, then appropriate, proportionate, and effective intervention or control measures can be introduced. Control measures are effectively the approaches to be taken to manage the risks identified in the community impact assessment. As with any risk assessment, the community impact assessment should be viewed as a "snapshot" in time and must be kept under constant review, reassessed, and the control measures altered as the assessed risk level changes.

The control measures adopted to mitigate the actual or perceived risks can be led by the community, interagency, or law enforcement. We suggest that best practice involves a multiagency response, including the community itself, as control measures may need to be carried out at different levels, some within the task of law enforcement and others more under control of the respective community. It is important to note, however, that because HBV may be committed with the active collusion of community members, any control measures that are community managed must be led by trusted community members.

Conducting a Community Impact Assessment

Before conducting any law enforcement operations, including arrest operations, it is important to measure the impact of the law enforcement operation on the wider or affected community. The processes involved in carrying out such a community impact assessment are identical to those that should be carried out in response to the occurrence of HBV. Essentially, information about the likely response of communities to law enforcement activity is located in the perceptions and attitudes of community members. As such, a community impact assessment necessarily relies upon the amount and accuracy of information that can be obtained from and about a community and the perceptions it holds.

Sources of Information

Information about communities can be obtained from a range of sources. These might include:

- Law enforcement and other social data that may give a general view of the sociodemographic breakdown of a community, as well as information concerning offending patterns in the area.
- Intelligence databases may be useful in detailing criminality and other threats to social order within the community.

While data of this sort provides general information about community risk factors, it may not provide sufficient detail to assess community responses to the occurrence of an HBV offense or to resultant law enforcement activity. Sources, such as *community police officers, community partners, strategic partners, not-for-profit organizations,* or *police informants* also may need to be consulted to establish what specifically may be taking place in the community. An important caveat in collecting information to aid an assessment is its reliability, and it is important for assessors to consider the source and nature of information in making such judgments.

EEP Model for Community Impact Assessment

As a general guide to conducting a community impact assessment, we have reproduced below the London MPS model. This model for conducting community impact assessments is referred to as the EEP model with the letters in the abbreviation referring to Experienced, Evidenced, and Potential. Experienced refers to an assessment of how a community feels about a particular event or events. Evidenced refers to an assessment of relevant law enforcement information about what is happening in the community. Potential refers to making an assessment on the basis of this information of what might happen in the future. The EEP model describes various sources of information that need to be considered in making a community impact assessment and provides guidance on the identification of possible scenarios concerning what may happen. A risk level is then attributed to various outcomes. Below we describe the sorts of information that needs to be considered in making the assessment following the EEP framework:

- **Experienced**: This part of the assessment is designed to gauge how a community feels concerning a particular event. The information relevant to making this assessment will be obtained from a diverse range of sources that may include:
  - Any community-based advisory group
  - Not-for-profit organizations with interests in a community
  - Youth group leaders
  - Faith groups
  - Community rumor
  - Community intelligence
  - Social networks, e.g. Facebook, Twitter, etc.
  - Open source media, e.g., national or local newspapers
  - Specialist publications aimed at specific communities
  - Key community networks
  - Debriefs of community police officers
- **Evidenced**: This part of the assessment concerns consideration of the information that law enforcement have available to them concerning what is happening within a community. This includes consideration of:
  - Information from experience patrol and community police officers
  - Law enforcement investigators within the community
  - Information held by law enforcement, e.g., calls for assistance, stop/searches
  - Reported crimes in the area
  - Criminal intelligence concerning the area
- **Potential**: This refers to an assessment of what has the potential to happen within a community. This will include consideration of:
  - The impact of any planned or predicted events by law enforcement and other agencies within the community
  - Significant anniversaries and other events likely to have an impact, e.g., murders, funerals, festivals, significant international events

Community Risk Assessment and Management

Having considered a range of information and to determine possible events that may occur within a community, it is important to consider their likelihood. This is essentially a risk assessment similar to that carried out for victims of HBV.

If a particular community outcome is identified, e.g., violence, in response to law enforcement action to arrest a perpetrator of HBV, the assessment considers how likely this is to occur on the basis of the available information. In using the EEP model, there are six risk assessment levels that are based on the likelihood and imminence of occurrence of an event. They include:

- Imminent (level 1), an event that is very likely to occur in the near future
- High
- Moderate (high)
- Moderate (low)
- Above Normal
- Normal (level 6), an event that is no more likely to occur in the current circumstances

In managing a particular risk, various strategies or control measures need to be put in place. The type of control measures employed will be determined by the level of risk and the likely impact of the measure upon the community. So, for example, it may be judged that the risk of protest and violence within the community is imminent in the event of an arrest of a perpetrator for HBV. The control measures employed, therefore, may involve consideration of the timing of the arrest, engagement with community leaders to explain the necessity of the arrest, involvement of NGOs in outreach to community members, and the involvement of sufficient law enforcement resources to affect the arrest and to police the community to avoid and violence. Of course, the control measures selected will be determined on a case-by-case basis reflecting the assessed risk. It is important to note that any control measure will itself have an impact upon the community and this needs to be carefully considered and also further illustrates that any risk assessment process is not a one-off event, but needs to be ongoing.

Community Consultation

Community consultation is an important aspect of any assessment. Indeed the involvement of the community can in itself be seen as a control measure, it demonstrates a desire to involve communities, and giving a voice to communities is a central part of law enforcement maintaining legitimacy in the eyes of a community (Tyler, 2006). In fact, within most Western nations, policing is by consent and most policing service delivery plans involve community engagement as a central feature. Therefore, community consultation should not be seen as an example of appeasement or political correctness, but part of more general policing strategies; certainly, communities are frequently the experts in the best ways to manage risks within themselves.

Conclusion

This chapter has explored risk assessment and risk management within HBV, and we have noted that effective risk assessment and management strategies are a way in which victims, witnesses, and the community may be protected from harm. It is important to note that while making informed decisions, those involved in risk management must accord the victim a clear voice in the decision making; working together with victims and being sensitive to their needs and wishes will aid risk management significantly. This similarly applies to the community, as having an open dialog with communities will enhance the ability of law enforcement to manage community risks. Finally, in considering risk management, it is important to note that inaction by law enforcement and other agencies can have tragic consequences for victims, potentially leading to forced marriage, rape, false imprisonment, or even homicide, and, for communities, potentially resulting in failing relationships with law enforcement and even community discord and violence. It is vital that agencies are prepared and ready to thoroughly assess and manage the risks in suspected HBV cases.

In the next chapter, we move on to consider an important aspect of the investigation and management of HBV cases multiagency working and how this can be best achieved.

Multiagency Working and Honor-Based Violence

8

So far, we have discussed at length the role of law enforcement in dealing with honor-based violence (HBV) and we have pointed out that it is important for law enforcement to work with other agencies. Multiagency working can be problematic as different agencies bring different procedures and expectations to the table. This can have negative consequences for victims and witnesses of HBV because different procedures may potentially expose them to risk. Therefore, it is imperative that all agencies concerned with HBV develop protocols to facilitate interagency working. In this section, we will explore the responsibilities of other agencies as regards HBV and will suggest approaches that might facilitate efficient interagency cooperation.

Developing Strategies

To facilitate agencies in developing procedures, some legislatures have produced statutory guidance for dealing with HBV. For example, in the United Kingdom the government (2009) has produced a document, *Multi-Agency Practice Guidelines: Handling Cases of Forced Marriage*. It was developed alongside the statutory guidance that was issued under s.63 Q(1) Forced Marriage Civil Protection Act 2007. It sets out the responsibilities of chief executives, directors, and senior managers within agencies involved with handling forced marriage cases and reiterates the importance a truly multiagency response. This guidance is applicable to managing other forms of HBV as well.

HBV Lead Officer

We stress that it is important for agencies to clearly identify an individual who is their lead on HBV related matters. This person should receive training and staff development in HBV and should act as an organizational resource on HBV matters. It is important that other members of the organization are clear on who this person is and what this person's responsibilities are as well as how he/she may be contacted. The organization, therefore, should design procedures for involving the HBV lead where HBV is suspected or detected.

In general, most agencies will have a lead individual who has responsibilities for safeguarding children and protecting vulnerable adults or victims of domestic abuse. Following from the issues discussed within this book, e.g., the incidence of HBV against the vulnerable or the young, we argue that it would be consistent with these responsibilities for this person also to include HBV within his portfolio and be recognized as the agency lead on matters related to HBV. Such a person is likely to have many of the requisite skills and knowledge to manage an agency's response to HBV, recognizing, in particular, the issues faced by vulnerable individuals and the needs for resourcing and training within an agency.

An HBV lead is probably the minimum an agency will require to respond effectively to HBV. In the sections below, we consider recommended responses for different statutory agencies.

Health Professionals

Health professionals should recognize that, although victims may not present HBV directly to them, they are in an ideal position to provide early assistance and intervention. A meeting with a health professional may be the only opportunity that a victim of HBV has of disclosing her concerns in a safe and protected environment.

Healthcare environments should attempt to create an environment in which HBV can be discussed openly and victims of HBV will have the confidence to know they will be listened to and believed. Victims attending health environments, such as hospitals, health clinics, or local physician offices should feel reassured about their confidentiality. Health environments also could consider making available time slots and situations where HBV victims can have opportunities to talk openly and freely about any concerns they have.

Open and supportive services can be achieved by displaying relevant information and posters in appropriate languages, educating health professionals on HBV-related issues, circulating relevant literature to target audiences in a sensitive and appropriate manner, and involving survivors and affected communities in training staff.

Many HBV victims will assume that health professionals will not be able to help them and, therefore, will not present to them as a victim of HBV. This often stems from their experiences in their home country where some health professionals may be supportive of HBV or from lack of knowledge and understanding of the role and ability of healthcare professionals to offer support.

Training of healthcare staff also should include training in sensitive and appropriate questioning methods to enable them to obtain relevant information from victims should HBV be suspected. Health professionals also should be confident and able to refer HBV victims on to other agencies, such as law enforcement, social services, or nongovernment organizations (NGOs) with expertise in HBV, in particular being aware of who to contact and how to contact them.

Ultimately health professionals may have to make difficult decisions concerning HBV and the victim. To make their decision-making process less onerous, it is very important that health professionals are supported by their managers and have access to HBV specialists who can advise on appropriate responses.

If after appropriate and sensitive questioning, a health professional feels that there is a real and imminent threat to a person's well being, then processes should be in place so that the health professional can access relevant support quickly to protect the victim. How this will be achieved will vary from jurisdiction to jurisdiction and will be dependent on the multiagency working practices in place. However, it is very important that law enforcement agencies develop close working arrangements with health professionals so that they are able to quickly intervene should health professionals identify an immediate risk of violence to a victim.

Education

Often teachers, lecturers, or other educational staff members are in a position to recognize HBV victimization. This is often because they will see various behavioral changes of HBV victims. For example, they may see *withdrawal from education, impaired social development, depression and self-harming as well as failing educational achievement.* Other more specific issues that may come to light are *truanting, absenteeism from lessons, failure to take part in extra curricular activities, being accompanied by a chaperone such as another relative to and from school and even in break periods, as well as failing to complete set work or failure to achieve required educational standards.* Identifying these issues may allow education professionals to seize the opportunity to speak with victims and to listen to and address any concerns they may have. Taking such an opportunity can be very important in cases of HBV as discussing educational issues with a victim may be a legitimate way of approaching her that does not appear to be oppressive or intimidating to the victim and provides the victim with perhaps the only opportunity she may have to speak of her concerns to someone outside of her family.

A key issue that educational staff may face is where a student discloses that she is due to go on a family overseas holiday for a prolonged period of time. Frequently, in cases of HBV where forced marriage is concerned, a family wedding may be mentioned as the reason for the overseas trip. Where HBV is an issue, the wedding in question may be the student's own wedding, although she may not be aware of this. It is particularly important to note that the student may be being taken overseas to marry even if she is below the age of consent for the jurisdictions. Of course, it also is very important not to simply assume on the basis of a child's cultural or religious heritage that a planned trip overseas for a wedding is an example of a forced wedding. A forced wedding is more likely where the trip is associated with other observed behavioral changes in the student or child of the type described above. It is vitally important that educational staff, when presented with information of this type, consider the possibility that what is being reported may be HBV and to report this to the appropriate person or agency. As mentioned above, schools should identify an HBV lead with whom this suspicion should be discussed.

Though the signs described above are indicators that something may be wrong, it is only through appropriate and sensitive questioning that education professionals may identify the cause of the problem. Therefore, it is appropriate to create an open environment where students will feel safe to discuss the problems they are facing, knowing they will be listened to and their concerns will be taken seriously.

Educational establishments can create an open and supportive environment in respect to HBV by circulating information leaflets, displaying relevant information on HBV, having in place the availability of a telephone to enable students to seek advice discreetly, educating staff about the issues of HBV, and the presenting symptoms. Also, having referral systems in place so that students can talk to an appropriate professional who can provide practical and realistic advice and are cognizant of HBV issues, as well as introducing HBV into the curriculum, which could include making available to students books and films about HBV and its causes and effects.

It is important that once educational staff has established that HBV is a concern, advice should be offered to the student regarding contacts for specialist advice and guidance. Where an HBV lead exists, the student should be referred to that staff member. Child protection legislation may be relevant in cases where a student is legally a child within the laws of a particular region.

Where the level of concern is high and there is felt to be a real and imminent risk to the welfare of the student, then the education professional should seek further advice from his/her HBV lead as well as immediately contacting appropriate partner agencies.

It is important that law enforcement agencies work closely with their educational partners so that a coordinated response to HBV can be developed. Law enforcement agencies need to recognize how educational establishments work with their students and to utilize the unique student–teacher relationships that prevail. This can be an obvious opportunity for law enforcement to have access to victims in a safe and controlled environment where family members are less able to influence the interaction or threaten the victim.

Educational professionals also can be the eyes and ears for a multiagency response where suspected HBV has been identified. They may identify changes in circumstances that may have a significant effect upon risk assessment and relevant safety plans that have been put in place. It is incumbent on law enforcement agencies to be proactive in developing close, effective professional relationships with educational establishments that are mutually beneficial to the respective educational institution, the law enforcement agency, and, of course, the victim herself.

Children's Social Services

We have already mentioned HBV and children, though this is discussed more extensively in later chapters. Where children are victims or potential victims of HBV, it is essential that children's social services play a key role in protecting the interests of the child. Although children's social services need to be sensitive to cultural and racial differences, their overriding duty is protecting children and young people from harm.

Where children's social services are the first contact point by a victim, it is imperative that the group gathers as much information as possible in an appropriate and sensitive way. It is a recognized policy among many children's social services to mediate with families or contact them directly where child protection issues are felt to be relevant to a particular family. However, we strongly argue that, in cases of HBV, this should *not be done* nor should social services challenge the family with respect to HBV issues. This is because of the substantial risks of harm faced by victims that can be compounded if a family is informed or confronted about suspected HBV. The response to HBV has to be a multiagency joint response in which law enforcement takes primacy in contacting the family. Law enforcement has the skills and resources to minimize risks to victims, in particular, through arrest of individuals who act in a threatening manner; these are powers that agencies, such as social services, do not have. If the threat of harm toward a victim is imminent, then law enforcement must be involved as soon as possible.

Children's social services also may be informed of HBV via a third party. In these circumstances, we advocate contacting law enforcement and invoking a multiagency response to assess the risk posed to the victim. As with all HBV cases, confidentiality and discretion are vitally important.

The involvement of law enforcement is particularly important where there may be a need to liaise with international and overseas organizations in forced marriage or female genital mutilation (FGM) allegations. It is important to note that where information is shared with overseas organizations, agencies need to ensure that the information does not inadvertently place someone else in danger, such as previous or current boyfriends, friends, etc.

In the event that a child has contacted social services from overseas, perhaps fearing for her life or that she is or has been forced into a marriage, it is important that she is reassured that everything will be done to return her to her home country. There will then be a need to work with the appropriate government agencies to locate and repatriate the child. This process may be complicated if the child or young person holds dual nationality, making her a citizen of not only her homeland but also the country in which she is now being held. The process also will be further complicated if the country in which the child or young person is being held does not have or has limited diplomatic relationships with the home country of the victim. We recommend contacting government agencies in your jurisdiction with expertise in these issues, e.g., the Foreign Office Forced Marriage Unit (FMU) in the United Kingdom, when an HBV victim is overseas.

When a child is repatriated to her home country, we recommend that children's social services play a key role in receiving the child and undertaking the practical support that she will need upon her return.

Adult Social Services

Many actions by adult social care workers will be dependent on local legislation and the local structures that are in place. However, we argue that social services available to adult victims of HBV should be similar to those for any other victim of HBV. It is important that victims have access to knowledgeable staff able to provide confidential support and guidance, and who are familiar with local legislation. As with other social services, adult services should develop close working procedures with law enforcement and have the ability to involve law enforcement at an early stage following discovery of suspected HBV.

Vulnerable Adults

Adults with intellectual or learning difficulties, physical disabilities, and/or mental health issues may be highly vulnerable to HBV, in particular, forced marriage. This is because they often lack the capacity to consent to marriage and are dependent on their family for their support needs. Without a doubt, for some families, having a child with a vulnerability of this kind challenges their family honor and, thus, it is important to force the child into marriage to restore honor by showing that their child is desirable as a marriage partner. Marriage in the case of vulnerable daughters also will have the effect of shifting any financial burden onto the family of her husband. For marriages of this sort, parents will often accept a spouse that they would normally consider unacceptable in order to facilitate a marriage.

The measures in place for vulnerable adults with support needs should be the same as for any adult HBV victim, although agencies involved in protecting adults with support needs should also recognize that they will need additional support to ensure the victim's safety and protection, including the opportunity to be able to talk to a member of social services who is able to engage with the victim in a manner that is appropriate to his/her particular needs. It is important that, where HBV is suspected or has occurred in relation to a vulnerable adult, then an adult social care worker discusses with the individual the range of options available and the possible consequences of those actions.

Many of the other issues we have raised with children and young persons above also are applicable to vulnerable adults, notably around dealing with third-party informants, victims located in a foreign country, and repatriation, as well as contacting and mediating with the victim's family.

For vulnerable adults, it is particularly important that social service staff can provide:

- Reassurance that their concerns will be listened too
- Information so that they know how to raise concerns with people
- Insurance that they have access to adults outside of the family

It is important that, regardless of the allegation made by vulnerable adult victims of HBV, social services provide practical and possibly financial help to support them in their decision-making processes if they have the mental capacity to make such decisions. Working with partners, it should be the aim of adult social services to ensure the victims are safe, the risk of harm to them is managed, and, where criminal offenses are identified, the victims are supported through any criminal justice process.

Conclusions

In this chapter, we have considered the responsibilities of agencies other than law enforcement in responding to HBV and have made a number of suggestions that might help facilitate the early identification of HBV and efficient interagency working. Ultimately, it is essential that all agencies dealing with HBV work with the same principles so as to facilitate the best possible service to victims. It also is important that, where agencies have not responded appropriately, these failings need to be identified and challenged, and support provided to ensure the agency in question recognizes the failings and improves their processes.

In the next chapter, we move on to consider effective methods for agencies to communicate information about HBV.

Communication Strategies

9

There has been much prolonged discourse in the academic literature about what constitutes honor-based violence (HBV) and we have provided something of this debate in Chapter 1. These debates draw into sharp focus some of the difficulties authorities and individuals have in identifying HBV. One particular problem is that many agencies and individuals don't recognize when an individual has suffered HBV victimization. In addition, for many individuals, even recognition of their own victimization does not guarantee that they will report it to the relevant authorities. This makes the task of investigation of offenses and prevention of HBV very difficult as authorities may be unaware of the true extent of HBV-related incidences and, therefore, unable (or unwilling) to respond appropriately.

How then should authorities, such as law enforcement, respond to these problems? Clearly for authorities to be able to adequately deal with incidents of HBV, they need to be able to identify them, and victims need to feel confident in reporting them. In this regard, the manner in which HBV-related information is communicated to the broader community is of some importance. This chapter will explore the issue of communication, looking particularly at how messages about HBV may be communicated by authorities, including law enforcement, to various stakeholders and the impact of different communication strategies. We also will stress the importance of authorities communicating unequivocal, united, and consistent messages to stakeholders concerning the definition of and their actions toward HBV. We argue that, only with such communication will victims be able to identify their victimization, feel more confident in the type of treatment they will receive from an authority, and thus feel more comfortable in reporting victimization. Likewise, authorities will be able to ensure that their staff members are aware of HBV and how the authority plans to deal with it.

Barriers to Reporting HBV

In considering an appropriate communication strategy, it is useful first to consider some of the barriers to reporting HBV experienced by victims. We have mentioned some of these previously, but it is worth considering them again in this context. These include:

- Fear of not being believed
- Previous negative experience with police and other professionals, e.g., social services
- Fear of law enforcement and government agencies
- Fear that children will be taken into the care of the state
- Fear for their own future, e.g., where the victim has a disability and a perpetrator is a caregiver
- Fear of deportation, particularly if she/he has insecure immigration status
- Fear of criminalization of self or other family members
- Fear that their religion will be portrayed negatively or otherwise vilified
- Fear of putting other people at risk, e.g., female relatives
- Language barriers
- Fear of retribution against self or family
- Lack of understanding of entitlements
- Fear of the unknown, i.e., what will happen next
- Social and financial dependence on the abuser(s)
- Belief that victims have brought shame on themselves, their family, and/or community
- Fear that their lifestyle will become public knowledge, e.g.. lesbian, gay, bisexual, and transgender (LGBT)

A perusal of this list illustrates that a major barrier to reporting is a victim's fear and uncertainty about what will happen to him/her. It is suggested, therefore, that an important aspect of any communication should be an attempt to explain what HBV is, an authority's responses to it, and to reassure victims and potential victims that they will be believed.

Stakeholders to Whom Communication Is Directed

In considering communication strategies, it is important to give consideration to the target of the message. With respect to HBV, it is suggested that there are four key stakeholder categories to which authorities, such as law enforcement and other statutory bodies, communicate messages concerning HBV. These include:

- Victims and prospective victims
- Perpetrators and prospective perpetrators
- Professionals, including law enforcement, education, housing officials, social workers, health workers, midwives, general practitioners, and emergency room medical staff
- Members of the community

All of these stakeholders are individuals who may come into contact with HBV and its aftermath and for whom knowledge about its characteristics and how authorities will deal with it is vital.

In the following sections, we explore best practice for communication strategies by considering the sorts of messages that should be communicated to the various stakeholders.

Key Messages

The characteristics of communicated messages are highly influential upon the impact of the message upon the recipient (Ajzen, 1992). In general, influential messages are consistent, clear, and unambiguous in the information that they provide. This generally means that the communicated message is easy for the recipients to follow and understand. It is vitally important that, when communicating key messages, careful consideration is given to the terminology that is used in the message so as to have maximum influence upon the target audiences, i.e., one or more of the five notable categories identified above. To achieve this, the messages communicated need to use *simple, unambiguous language* that is easy to understand, be *consistent* so that authorities communicate the same messages from all parts of their organization, and offer *clear recommendations and directions* to the recipient regarding possible courses of action. We suggest, as best practice, that authorities should attempt to communicate the following messages to all stakeholders:

- A clear and unambiguous definition of what honor-based violence is, making it clear that it is fundamentally an abuse of the human rights of women, men, and children.
- A statement that HBV involves serious crimes, which are likely to worsen over time potentially culminating in serious injury or death of the victim.

We also recommend that in addition, authorities communicate key sections of relevant domestic and international legislation. This helps to anchor anti-HBV messages within a national and international legislative framework, illustrating how these acts are an abuse of human rights as well as illegal activities. Relevant international legislation includes:

- Article 16(1) & (2) of the Universal Declaration of Human Rights (1948).
  - (1) Men and women of full age, without any limitation due to race,
    - Nationality or religion, have the right to marry and to found a family.

- They are entitled to equal rights as to marriage, during marriage and at its dissolution.
  - (2) Marriage shall be entered into only with the free and full consent of the intending spouses.
- Article 34 United Nations Convention on the Rights of the Child.
  - Children should be protected from all forms of sexual exploitation including unlawful sexual activity.
- General Recommendation 21, Comment Article 16(1)(b) United Nations Convention on the Elimination of All Forms of Discrimination Against Women.
- A woman's right to choose a spouse and enter freely into marriage is central to her life and her dignity and equality as a human being.

Key Messages to Victims of HBV

It is very important that all authorities recognize that their communications do have a significant impact upon both victims and prospective victims of HBV. Clear and consistent messages, therefore, are likely to aid victims in recognizing their victimization and to reassure them that there is something that they can do about it. As regards victims, we recommend the following as best practice within a communication strategy:

- It is important that there is a clear statement regarding which agencies victims should contact or approach including relevant contact details.
- The communication must give recipients confidence that they will be believed and that positive action will be taken following a report of HBV.
- Emergency telephone and helpline numbers should be provided, including the emergency number for local law enforcement agencies, given that some victims are likely to be children or from overseas who may be unfamiliar with these numbers.
- Communications should specify what action law enforcement or other officials will take if an honor-based violence matter is reported to them. For example, *all enquiries will be treated in the strictest of confidence and in a sensitive manner, that victim safety is a priority, and that steps will be taken to ensure this, and that victims will be put into contact with specialist agencies who have staff from diverse cultures, nationalities, and faith groups with a range of linguistic skills who will provide help and advice.* This is likely to help reassure victims that there is someone who can offer help and who will believe them. This also helps to challenge some of the barriers to reporting HBV considered above.

- Communication strategies also should seek to provide crime prevention and personal safety advice because some individuals may be unable or unwilling to contact authorities. This may be the only advice they will receive about how to protect themselves.

Key Messages to Perpetrators

The statements made by authorities also are communications with perpetrators or would-be perpetrators of HBV. As such, the messages communicated by the authority should be consistent and clearly articulate its policies towards HBV. As examples of best practice, we recommend that the following messages should be communicated:

- HBV is not acceptable behavior.
- HBV is taken very seriously by the authorities and is treated as serious crime.
- HBV cases will be thoroughly investigated.
- Perpetrators will be arrested and prosecuted and may go to prison.
- By committing such crimes, perpetrators will bring dishonor on themselves, their family, and community.

It is also important to communicate with those who may consider recruiting others to commit HBV and illustrate to them that such activity is treated very seriously. A communication strategy should include statements to the effect that if you ask, persuade, or force someone to commit an HBV crime or are involved in any way, no matter how small, you commit a very serious criminal offense.

Likewise, it is important to communicate to those who may be asked to be involved in HBV with messages such as, if you are approached to commit crime, you must report this to law enforcement.

Key Messages for Professionals

A communication strategy should recognize that among key stakeholders are various professionals, such as health, social, youth, education, and other services, who may come into contact with victims or perpetrators of HBV. It is important to note that such contact may be the only time a victim speaks to a third party about her experiences and this may be the only opportunity for intervention. It is important that professionals recognize what HBV is and feel empowered to act on a victim's behalf. As best practice, we, therefore, recommend that communication strategies need to state clearly:

- Victims of HBV have a fundamental right to be listened to and to be believed.
- Professionals should take positive action on every occasion where HBV is suspected.
- Professionals should not think that it is someone else's job and turn victims away.
- All information provided by a victim must be handled with sensitivity and in the strictest of confidence.
- Professionals should not make value judgments about the victim, her family, and/or community.
- Professionals should manage victims in a culturally sensitive way.
- Professionals should interact with the victims in an empathetic and sympathetic manner.
- Professionals should not underestimate the potential risk of harm for a victim.
- HBV victimization is not confined to particular communities; it can involve victims of both genders, as well as adults and children.
- HBV victimization can involve individuals from different cultures, e.g., where an individual is romantically involved with someone from a different religion, nationality, or culture.
- Professionals, if in doubt, should seek advice as soon as practicable and while the victim or concerned person is still with them.
- Organizations must put checks and balances in place to ensure that victim's details are secure and that there is no unauthorized access to victim's personalized data.

Key Messages to Communities

Some members of the community may regard HBV as an acceptable cultural practice that will be tolerated by those in authority. It is important that this perception is challenged because changing community attitudes of this kind is an important first step to minimizing the risk of HBV. A communication strategy can help to reduce the likelihood of HBV by stressing that it is unacceptable and regarded by authorities, especially law enforcement, as a serious crime. We, therefore, recommend that a communication strategy should include these statements:

- Honor-based violence involves serious crimes committed against defenseless victims.
- HBV-related offenses against children are regarded as child abuse.
- The commission of HBV crimes brings dishonor on a community.
- HBV crimes also amount to a serious abuse of human rights.

- It is the civic duty of community members to challenge this criminal conduct and report it to the authorities.
- If members of the community hear or see threats or intimidating behavior, they have a duty to report these to the authorities, making clear which authorities, e.g., law enforcement, should be informed and how they should be informed including relevant telephone numbers.

We also suggest that a communication strategy should stress that community members should not ignore HBV, assume that it is none of their business, or wait for someone else to report it to authorities. It is important to stress that individuals, if in doubt, should always report their concerns to the authorities. It is important as well to stress that the actions of community members can save lives and/or improve a victim's quality of life.

Methods of Communication

In communicating messages to various stakeholders, it is important to consider the various methods of communication that may be used. As previously stated, it is essential that consistent key messages are developed and communicated in an effective way, which ensures that this penetrates communities and reaches the eyes and ears of all stakeholders. In order to achieve this, authorities must tailor and adapt their messages to the characteristics of the audience. Consideration also needs to be given to the most appropriate delivery method that will maximize the impact of the message, ensuring that it is not diluted and that it reaches the widest possible audience.

Communication Media

There are a wide range of communication media and the selection of the most appropriate will depend upon who the target audience is and budgetary restrictions. Wide-ranging campaigns may utilize several media, such as press, Internet, Facebook, Twitter, leaflet campaigns, etc. Smaller, more targeted campaigns may involve face-to-face meetings with community members or targeted leaflets aimed at relevant stakeholders. Below is a breakdown of various media that may be used to various extents:

- National and local media (TV, radio, and newspapers)
- Minority ethnic publications (including TV, radio, newspapers)
- Mainstream women's publications
- Internet marketing
- Web sites of statutory services providers
- Community events

- Religious establishments
- School, college, or university events
- Leaflets and other publicity material posted in areas where the recipients of the message may be in waiting rooms, e.g., doctor's offices
- Text messaging at events, e.g., use of Bluetooth technology
- Use of the Internet and social media

It is important given the likely diverse nature of the recipients of messages that information is produced in accessible formats especially in a variety of languages dependent on the target audience and in formats accessible to disabled community members.

Manner of Communication

With HBV, it is important that consideration is given to the mode, manner, and place of communication because it is possible to unwittingly place victims at risk of violence. For example, a victim may be subject of an HBV attack for having a leaflet about HBV in his/her possession. As such, there may be situations in which certain types of information are not appropriate.

Who Should Communicate Messages?

No communicated message appears in a vacuum; instead, it appears within a particular sociocultural context. The context consists of factors, such as *who* is making the communication, their *characteristics*, the *purpose of the communication,* and the *characteristics of the audience* (Ajzen, 1992). The characteristics of the source of the communication are particularly influential in the ability of the message to influence (in the direction intended) the recipients. Therefore, as well as considering the contents of a communication and the most appropriate mode of delivery, authorities also need to give consideration to who is going to deliver the messages.

The characteristics of the communicator are referred to in social psychology as *source factors*. These include biological attributes, such as race, age, height, and gender; behavioral features that include the manner in which the communicator delivers a message if it is done in real time, such as mannerisms, facial expressions, hand and body movements, and social features including the perceived social status of the communicator, level of self-confidence, and perceived power. Of importance, however, are the perceived (by the audience) credibility and attractiveness to the audience of the communicator (Ajzen, 1992).

Credibility is associated with the extent to which the audience believes that the communicator is trustworthy and has sufficient expertise to comment upon the issue. To say this in another way, does the communicator have the knowledge to provide information and, if so, can he/she be trusted to provide all of the relevant information in an unbiased manner? Generally, as credibility increases, the power of the message to persuade increases; this means that authorities, when communicating messages on HBV, should be very sensitive to the perceived credibility of the communicator (Ajzen, 1992).

Attractiveness is associated with the physical, gender, and experiential characteristics of the communicator. While attractiveness is associated with lay perceptions of what an attractive person is like, it is more than this and refers to the extent to which the audience judges the communicator as being attractive as a communicator. Attractiveness as a communicator relates strongly to the extent an individual is similar to the audience in terms of background, characteristics, and experience. Messages tend to have greater impact if an audience perceives the communicator as being attractive and similar to them (Ajzen, 1992).

Clearly then, different audiences will have different perceptions as to what constitutes a credible and attractive communicator. So, as examples, communicating messages concerning HBV to nurses or doctors might best be achieved using individuals who have medical training and expertise. In contrast, providing messages about law enforcement responses to HBV may best be provided by a senior police officer who may be perceived as having authority and expertise in HBV and the law. Communications to victims concerning the types of support available may best be achieved by victims of HBV who tell of their experiences; such individuals may readily be perceived as having expertise in HBV, as being similar to other victims in their experience and characteristics, and may be persuasive sources of information about what victims should do. Similarly, religious and other community leaders may be persuasive communicators when presenting information, which accords with the authorities' key messages to other community members about HBV.

Ultimately, the selected communicator will depend on the target audience at the particular time. Below is a list of the types of communicator that can be considered:

- Survivors of honor-based violence
- Government ministers
- Male and female role models from affected communities, e.g., members of the government who hold high office, members of Congress, House of Representatives, other senior professionals, movie/sports and music industry stars
- Senior law enforcement officers and their professional counterparts
- Religious leaders
- Not-for-profit/nongovernment organizations (NGOs) representing women and men who have experienced honor-based violence or threats of it

Conclusion

In this chapter, we have considered communication strategies and provided some advice regarding best practice. It is essential that authorities give consideration to the messages that they present regarding HBV and effective means of directing these messages to the intended recipients. As we discussed, there are a range of different audiences each with their own needs and perceptions and messages; if they are to be influential, they need to be cognizant of these. Similarly, the means of communication is influential as some may fail to reach intended audiences or may be inappropriate for their needs. Finally, the characteristics of the communicator are important and authorities need to consider who will provide the message and the extent to which such individuals are likely to be regarded by the specific audience as credible and attractive presenters. Ultimately, well-considered communication strategies that provided targeted information in appropriate formats that is consistent and easy for an audience to understand can have a significant impact upon reducing the likelihood of HBV and providing victims with the necessary information needed to escape violence. In the next chapter, we move on to discuss children and HBV.

Children and Honor-Based Violence

10

In this book, we have discussed at length the causes and extent of honor-based violence (HBV), and how it affects individuals, families, and communities. However, we believe that it is important to consider separately HBV as it affects children and the approaches to intervention. To preempt much of what we will argue, we suggest that agencies should design responses specifically for child victims of HBV. This is because child victims present a number of additional challenges (as compared with adults) that are associated with their psychological and physical vulnerability and that, in many cases, they are reliant upon their abusers to care for them. This chapter will explore child HBV victimization and its characteristics, and will present some suggestions for best practice in dealing with and preventing its occurrence.

Age

Before further discussion, it is necessary to define what we mean by a *child*. For the purposes of this book, a child is defined as anyone less than 18 years of age. However, it must be noted that the legal definition of a "child" does vary dependent with jurisdiction, so readers should refer to their own relevant legislation for a definition. Regardless of how a child is defined, the principles we will discuss in this chapter will apply to protecting children suffering HBV.

Age and HBV Crime Type

It is important to note that some HBV crimes are more likely to occur when the victim is a child. For example, female genital mutilation (FGM) is most likely in very young children, perhaps because at these ages they are easier for adults to control. Forced marriage is more likely when children become adolescents. Adolescence is a particular key age for HBV because this is an age when many children may begin to challenge parental authority and family rules, particularly if they are exposed to a Western lifestyle. "Becoming too Westernized" is a frequently cited motive by perpetrators of HBV in Western nations.

Reporting Offenses

An important issue when considering child victimization is how law enforcement becomes aware of HBV. As with other forms of child abuse, concerns about a child may be raised to authorities from many sources including family members, schools, youth clubs, a child's friends, or from missing person reports. It is often the case, however, that issues related to HBV initially may not be reported as crimes. For example, bad behavior at school, truancy, prolonged absences from school, and/or being accompanied by a chaperone while at school can be associated with HBV victimization of children and may be observed by others, such as education professionals giving rise to their concern. What is important, regardless of how authorities are made aware of concerns about a child, is that a proper investigation into the circumstances takes place so that facts can be established quickly and so that relevant risks can be assessed.

Missing Persons

One way in which authorities frequently become aware of HBV-related issues involving children is through missing person reports. Children have many reasons for running away from home and, in an HBV context, we consider some of them below.

Motives for Running Away From Home

Where HBV is an issue, the motives for running away from home will reflect the fear of harm a child is experiencing. Commonly, the reasons for HBV child victims to run away from home include fear of forced marriage; physical and psychological abuse at home because the child is not adhering to family values and, therefore, dishonoring the family; to escape the stifling effects of a patriarchal community; nonacceptance of the child's sexuality; or running away with a boyfriend or girlfriend not approved of by the family.

Reporting Missing Children

Missing children may come to law enforcement notice in a number of different ways. A family may report a child missing because the child ran away from home, or a third party, such as friends or school teachers, may report the child missing. Below, we discuss the considerations and suggested responses of law enforcement depending on who makes a missing person report because this may be highly significant in cases of HBV.

Family Reports a Child Missing

Where HBV is an issue, family report of a missing child can have a number of motives. Some families may report a child missing (as they may with an adult) in order to utilize law enforcement as agents to discover the whereabouts of the child. This is often motivated by a desire to find the child so that they can be punished for dishonoring the family. Here the act of a child running away dishonors the family and honor may only be restored by the child being found and punished. In these circumstances, when a child is returned home, the child faces a significant risk of violence. Therefore, if there is any suspicion that a child has run away to avoid HBV, the primary concern should be the well being of the child and not the family.

If the child is found, it should *not be* a prerequisite that the child is returned home and the family *should not* be automatically informed of where the child is if that will place the child in danger. Only following a detailed consideration of all the circumstances, a full debrief with the missing child and other partner agencies, and on the completion of a comprehensive risk assessment should the family be told the child is safe and well. Law enforcement and other agencies need to recognize that, where HBV is suspected and depending on assessed risk to the child, it may not be appropriate to inform the family of the child's whereabouts at all.

Friends or Peers Report a Child Missing

Children also may be reported missing by friends, peers, boyfriends, or girlfriends. We suggest these cases will require a significant amount of investigation because these circumstances may indicate a serious criminal offense may have taken place. For example, in HBV offenses, kidnapping and false imprisonment prior to a forced marriage or even an honor killing can be the reason for a child to be missing.

Clearly, in cases of missing children, it is unusual for parents not to report the child missing. In these circumstances, therefore, law enforcement should carefully question why the child has been reported missing by a third party and not by their family. They should then establish from friends and acquaintances the background to the disappearance and whether there is any indication as to why the child has gone missing. Time here is of the essence to prevent significant harm coming to the child, and/or to capture the relevant perpetrators and to maximize evidential retrieval.

School Teachers, Youth Leaders, or Other Professionals Report Child Missing

Children also may be reported as missing by schools or other professional bodies if they fail to return following a school holiday or vacation or if they simply cease to attend school. Evidence (e.g., Centre for Social Cohesion,

2010) suggests that it is at the time of holidays that children are often forced into marriage and never return to school.

Again, in these circumstances, law enforcement should carefully question why the family has not reported the child missing or contacted a school with an explanation for the child's absence. When law enforcement receives a report of a missing child in these circumstances, this may indicate that the child has been a victim of forced marriage, taken abroad to affect FGM, or even become the victim of an honor killing. It is imperative that such reports are taken seriously and law enforcement endeavors to identify where the child has been taken, by whom, and when. Should the child be located abroad, further investigation will involve engagement with specialist units, such as the U.K. Foreign Office forced marriage unit and liaison with overseas law enforcement agencies.

False Allegations of Criminality

When a child goes missing from an HBV environment, rather than reporting them as missing, a family sometimes will may make a false allegation of criminality against the child, e.g., that the child has stolen expensive jewelry from the home and then went missing. Again the reason for the family making such an allegation is so that law enforcement will act as agents for the family in locating the victim. If it is suspected that this may be the case, this should be noted within any crime report. If this fact becomes known at a later date, say, upon arrest of the child, and the child indicates HBV issues as a reason for running away, then these matters must be investigated fully in line with the guidance provided in this book.

Avoiding Making Assumptions

We cannot emphasize enough the level of danger a missing child faces. Decisions made following a report of a missing child where HBV is suspected could be a matter of life or death.

It is important, however, to note that investigating officers should *not* simply assume because a family fits a certain racial or social profile that the case in question is an HBV issue. The authors have knowledge of missing person investigations that have been deemed as HBV-related based solely on the missing person's ethnic background and religion where this was not the case. This has unfortunately resulted in a mistrust and loss of confidence in law enforcement by that family and its wider community as well as causing tension between law enforcement and other agencies, notably nongovernment organizations (NGOs). Any child reported missing regardless of the family cultural, religious, or ethnic background requires appropriate, sensitive, and professional investigation to establish the full facts and identify evidence. If an investigation is to be flagged as potentially HBV, then this decision should be based upon evidence, and a sound rationale should be provided as to why a particular investigation is believed to be HBV.

HBV Incidents Involving Children

Having discussed how suspected HBV incidents involving children may come to the notice of authorities, we now move on to explore the types of incidents suffered by child victims. Previously in this book, we have discussed in some detail the offenses that characterize HBV and, thus, to prevent repetition, in this section we will confine discussion to aspects of the offense type and investigative considerations that apply specifically to children.

To begin this discussion, it is important to note first that any individual may abuse or neglect a child by inflicting harm and/or by failing to act to prevent harm. This is very significant with respect to HBV because, where HBV is perpetrated, family members, while not directly complicit in the abuse, often acquiesce to it and, as such, these individuals may share criminal responsibility with more active perpetrators.

Child Abduction

Abduction happens to both adults and children in HBV contexts. Abduction of children especially can be a prerequisite to forced marriage or used as a tool by family members to control a child, especially when a child has attempted to run away from home. It is also the case that some families will remove a child from their country of residence to their family's motherland during a law enforcement investigation.

Homicide

Honor killings have been discussed previously; suffice it to say that families will kill children to protect family honor and for minor transgressions of an honor code. In the United Kingdom, specific legislation not only accounts for homicide itself, but also for *causing* or *allowing* the death of a child or vulnerable adult. This piece of legislation is quite powerful as regards HBV because it is a means of holding to account members of the family and the broader household who have knowingly allowed or participated indirectly in the death of a child. Law enforcement should explore the legislation of its jurisdiction to identify similar useful legislation.

Female Genital Mutilation (FGM)

We have discussed this matter in earlier chapters, but readers need to be aware that this offense occurs particularly to young girls. In the United Kingdom, the legislation against FGM includes the offense of FGM itself and also the *aiding, abetting, counseling,* or *procuring* of the offense. Also in the United Kingdom, the offense is committed by *taking an individual abroad* with the *intention* of committing FGM. This is useful legislation for law enforcement in tackling FGM and, as with honor killings, law enforcement should explore its own jurisdiction's legislation to aid them.

Forced Marriages

Forced marriages have been discussed previously, but suffice it to say that families do force very young children into marriage either in their country of domicile or in a foreign country. Where a child mentions that he/she believes that he/she is going to be forced into a marriage, authorities should take this very seriously regardless of the age of the child. There should be a timely and appropriate intervention because children often become aware of an impending marriage very near to the marriage date. Although, as mentioned previously, it is predominantly girls what are forced into marriage, boys as well can be forced into marriage, notably where sexual orientation or disabilities are an issue.

Rape and Sexual Assault

In HBV, rape and sexual assault, where children are concerned, is most common following a forced marriage where a child is expected to have sexual intercourse with her new husband on the wedding night. The husband, in particular, may be many years older than his new wife and she may be unwilling to engage in sexual activity. The result of a refusal can be a physical assault and rape. In many cases, due to the age of a child, they are unable to legally consent to sexual intercourse.

As with adult offenses, rape of children also can been seen to occur prior to an honor killing in an attempt to dehumanize and humiliate the victim and this may involve several perpetrators. Homicide investigators should be aware of this and attempt to obtain full sexual swabs in a postmortem.

Domestic Violence

Within homes where HBV is practiced, there is a likelihood that children will be exposed to domestic violence as male members of the family exert power and control over female members. The abuse may take many forms, although it frequently includes a physical component. This may include hitting, shaking, throwing, poisoning, burning, scalding, drowning, suffocating, stabbing, excessive restraint, or otherwise causing physical harm to a child. In the case of HBV, such acts are used as a means of controlling the child's behavior in line with the wishes of the family and community. Physical abuse of children can culminate in honor killing. Investigators should not underestimate the level of physical abuse that perpetrators will inflict on children in the name of honor.

The failure to fully investigate any allegation of domestic violence may place children within the household in significant danger. It is important, therefore, where domestic abuse is investigated and honor issues are suspected, that *all children* within the house should be identified and spoken to. Details of the children should be taken and recorded so that appropriate risk assessments and management of the risk can be undertaken, as well as enabling this information to be shared with relevant partners. If it is felt that there is an immediate risk to the children, then they should be removed from the family home using the relevant legislation appropriate to that jurisdiction.

Emotional Abuse

Emotional abuse is the persistent emotional maltreatment of a child and consists of behaviors such as threats, insults, demeaning comments, social isolation, and the like. It can be argued that any form of abuse directed at a child will have a strong, emotionally abusive component; being physically abused by a parent, the fear and upset that this is likely to cause is likely to result in some emotional damage for a child. In this regard, many of the practices associated with HBV feature a high level of emotional abuse, e.g., constant policing, especially of female children's behavior, social isolation, insults and criticism of Westernized behavior, and the fear of forced marriage and/or FGM. Another element of emotional abuse that may affect children is observing the HBV-related abuse of their siblings, and even honor killings. Again, this is abusive in the sense that this challenges a child's view of appropriate behavior by adults toward children and may have significant impact upon the child's psychological development.

Child Neglect

Neglect of children is the persistent failure to meet the child's basic physical and/or psychological needs that often result in the serious impairment of the child's health or development. The key area of neglect for children suffering HBV is the failure to protect them from physical, emotional, or sexual harm. We would suggest that neglect in the context of HBV is a significant concern. This point is brought into sharp relief in the cases of child-forced marriage where parents and other senior family members know that the child will potentially be exposed to, at the very least, sexual assault and, potentially, quite significant physical harm. We also can see this in FGM practices where young girls are exposed to physical harm where close relatives do nothing to protect the child and often physically restrain the child to enable the procedures to be carried out.

Investigators need to be aware that this neglect is often a deliberate act to enable HBV crimes to take place to protect family honor. Those guilty of the neglect may not acknowledge what they are doing is wrong, but believe it is necessary as part of their culture or religion.

Historical Abuse

Adults may inform agencies of HBV abuse that they suffered in the past. Sometimes such disclosures may come about when the person in question is a victim of another crime, e.g., domestic violence or where it is known the perpetrator is being investigated for an offense such as HBV. Where there may still be children residing with the perpetrators, law enforcement, along with partner agencies, needs to carry out a full risk assessment and develop a detailed risk management plan to protect the children. Where HBV is believed to be an issue, given the high risk of harm to potential victims, there is a requirement for a proactive response to protect children, identify offenders, and hold those perpetrators to account.

Psychological and Physical Effects of HBV Abuse on Children

The effects of HBV on children can be devastating. The sorts of HBV incidents described above feature, at the very least, neglect and emotional abuse and, all too frequently, elements of physical and even sexual abuse. The long-term effects of this abuse upon children are well documented and may result in a number of psychological and medical problems. These can include mental health problems, such as low self-esteem, anxiety, eating disorders, and depression, social problems (such as difficulty in dealing with others and making friends), alcohol and drug problems in later life, a risk of violence and aggression, and an increased likelihood of a range of physical illnesses, some specific to the abuse, such as infections resulting from such practices as FGM (Arata et al., 2005).

We suggest that where HBV is recognized, the child is in danger of significant harm and the level of care and intervention by law enforcement and partners should reflect this. By the term *significant harm*, we mean the significant impairment of a child's normal physical, intellectual, emotional, social and/or behavioral development resulting from the experience of ill treatment themselves or witnessing the ill treatment of others.

Intervention

In this section, we will explore best practice for intervention in cases of child HBV victimization. In general, the principles discussed previously within this book also apply to child victims. As such, the strategies and considerations outlined in the *primary investigation* and *secondary investigation* chapters (3–6) should be followed by law enforcement and other investigators. However, in many jurisdictions, there are additional considerations when dealing with reports of child abuse, and here we highlight those that are pertinent to HBV.

Safety of a Child

In most jurisdictions where child abuse is suspected, the most important principle is the safety of the child and her protection from further harm. It is important, therefore, to note that protecting children is generally not the preserve of a single agency and that best practice in child protection involves a coordinated multiagency approach. This is especially so for HBV, given its complexities. No single agency should manage an allegation of or HBV crime in isolation.

Agencies Involved in HBV

As for adult victimization, to provide a truly effective and comprehensive response to child HBV, victimization will involve many statutory and possibly nonstatutory agencies with an interest in child protection. There are many circumstances where investigations are undertaken by social services, and law enforcement may not be involved beyond an initial information sharing or decision-making stage. A number of different agencies may be involved in child HBV cases and these include, although are not limited to:

- Law enforcement
- Social services
- Education
- Health professionals
- Local authorities
- Central government
- Nongovernment agencies

Multiagency Working

Multiagency working is as we have described best practice in child protection and in dealing with child HBV cases. However, this is not without its problems. Each agency involved will have its own structures and systems, and all agencies will have specific responsibilities when it comes to protecting a child, and these may act as a barrier to cooperation between agencies. It is important that agencies are clear about their respective responsibilities. As we discussed in Chapter 8, to ease these potential problems, it is best practice for all agencies to establish working arrangements and protocols that maximize cooperation, ideally prior to having to deal with a suspected case of HBV. Similarly, it is very important in any child HBV investigation that time should not be wasted in considering which agency has primacy over another, but to incorporate the responsibilities of all agencies into a single plan with the child's interests at the center.

What can be seen in many working relationships involving the investigation of crimes against children is some overlapping of the boundaries between each agency's function. Therefore, it is essential that agencies are cognizant of their statutory position without minimizing the importance of understanding the needs of the other agencies, and, most importantly, what is the best interests of the child and her safety.

Initial Assessment

When presented with a report of child HBV, there will need to be some form of initial assessment in line with local protocols. The aim of this assessment should be to identify the needs of the child and her wider family as well as the probable provision of services by appropriate partners. The involvement of law enforcement at this stage will depend on local working practices, but we suggest the lead should be taken by whichever agency has most experience and knowledge of HBV cases. If criminality is suspected, which will often be the case in HBV, law enforcement should take the lead.

All practitioners in children's services should have a standardized approach to conducting the assessment of a child's needs in the context of HBV, given the often unique circumstances of this type of investigation. There needs to be a holistic approach to the child's needs taking account of parents, family, caregivers, and environmental factors. This will allow practitioners to be better placed to formulate an appropriate and proportionate plan that has the child's best interests at heart.

Initial Multiagency Strategy Meeting

We suggest that where child HBV is suspected, an initial multiagency strategy meeting is convened at the earliest opportunity. Who manages these meetings will very much depend upon local protocols and practices. Within the United Kingdom, these initial multiagency strategy meetings are managed by a local government authority's children's social care department. Depending on the urgency of the situation, this strategy meeting may be in the form of a face-to-face meeting or a series of telephone conversations. Given the complexities of HBV, a face-to-face meeting is preferable, but if the risk is imminent, then an initial telephone conference will have to suffice before a more detailed and thorough face-to-face meeting takes place. Where there is any potential criminality suspected, law enforcement agencies should always attend these meetings.

The decision as to whether law enforcement agencies investigate allegations of criminality should be a matter for the law enforcement agencies to decide. Where they do not investigate any allegation of criminality, then a clear rationale should be recorded. As a general rule of thumb, given the high risk faced by victims, we feel that all allegations of HBV-related criminality, regardless of how minor the offense may seem, should be investigated by law enforcement.

Records of Meetings

All meetings should be recorded and actions agreed upon so that all agencies are left in no doubt as to their responsibilities and the requirements to undertake designated tasks. Local practices and protocols with respect to joint working should not prevent this from happening.

Gathering of Evidence

Where law enforcement undertakes a criminal investigation, it should take full responsibility for evidence gathering and all forensic investigative activities as highlighted earlier within this book. It may be relevant for social services or other partners to have access to the information garnered by law enforcement so that they can fulfill their own requirements as set by local protocols and/or legislation.

Interviewing of Child Victims

In addition to the investigative guidelines set out earlier in this book, we recommend that, when child victims and child witnesses are interviewed with respect to HBV, they are interviewed by specialist trained officers who have experience in interviewing children and, preferably, experience in HBV investigations. This will ensure that best evidence is captured and all relevant and pertinent points are covered in the interview. If no such officers are available and interviews are undertaken (this should only occur in exceptional circumstances where there is a need to act quickly in order to protect a child), then the interviews should be reviewed at the earliest opportunity by an experienced and competent officer so that any gaps in evidence or information are identified and these gaps can be closed. We recommend that it is good practice that any HBV interview is peer reviewed to ensure all points have been covered, risks identified, and evidence obtained in full.

Sharing of Information Between Agencies

We have noted in this chapter how it is essential for all HBV investigations to have a partnership approach and this requires the sharing of information between agencies to ensure the safety of the child. Agencies that share information, however, must be cognizant of local protocols and legislative guidelines applicable to that particular jurisdiction. It is often only when information is shared from a variety of sources and put together that the full risk to a child is known.

Drawing up a *memorandum of understanding* between partners is good practice. This will clearly set out what information can be shared, what happens to that information once it is shared and what the respective agency are able to do with the information. It should also set out how, when, and why information is shared.

Security of Information

Some information is confidential and should it become public may endanger sources, identify strategies, or endanger witnesses and victims. We suggest that information of this sort, e.g., from law enforcement indices or confidential sources, should only be shared with a nonprosecuting authority under the proviso that the receiving agency will not pass on the information to another party without the express permission of law enforcement. When information is passed on, it should be done via secure e-mail so that there is a timed and auditable record of data transfer. The only exception to this being where information is passed on in a strategy meeting, in which case it should be duly noted in the minutes. It is best practice for law enforcement to pass on only factual information as opposed to raw intelligence or other information.

Information that has come from a highly sensitive source should not normally be passed on. Only in the event that its use will prevent serious harm coming to a child should such information be shared, and this should be on the instruction of a senior police officer who has reviewed the possible effects of sharing it. The fact it has been disclosed should be fully recorded along with the reasons for sharing the information. It may well be that the information is shared with certain caveats to protect the source of the information.

To summarize, when law enforcement shares information, we recommend that the following considerations are made:

- Proportionality: Balancing the needs of the individual against the wider needs of society, given the circumstances of the case in question, is it appropriate that information is shared?
- Legality: Is there a legal basis in statute or case law to support sharing the information?
- Accountability: Can law enforcement actions be scrutinized to show why the reasons for sharing were recorded and the factors that effected the decision to share were appropriate? This also may include reasons for not sharing information.
- Necessity: Law enforcement may need to justify any infringement of rights when sharing information. In the case of children suffering HBV, this will generally be the safety and well being of the child/children in question.

HBV Child Protection Strategy Meetings

Where a criminal investigation has substantiated HBV concerns regarding child safety, then we recommend that a child protection strategy meeting between partner agencies be considered to enable professionals involved with the child to assess all the information and decide how best to safeguard and promote the welfare of the child in the long term. A child protection strategy meeting is in addition to the previously mentioned initial strategy meeting. In the initial strategy meeting, the focus is upon an initial response to allegations of HBV, whereas an HBV child protection strategy meeting aims to set and manage a strategy for the long term well being of the child where HBV has been identified.

How such a meeting will work will depend on local protocols and legislation. We intend to give some practical guidelines as to what a child protection strategy meeting may look like, which will include possible law enforcement responsibilities and activity required before, during, and after the meeting.

Purpose of Child Protection Strategy Meetings
Child protection strategy meetings should be designed with the following aims:

- To bring together and analyze information in a multiagency setting so that informed decisions can be made in protecting the child's well being and the capability of the family to protect the child from harm.
- To consider the evidence presented to the conference and make informed judgments as to the risk of harm faced by the child now and in the future.
- To decide what action is required to protect the child.

Timing the First Child Protection Strategy Meeting

The timing of an initial strategy meeting will be dependent upon when all pertinent and relevant information has been gathered to allow for informed decision making. However, in many HBV cases, the child will be at risk of significant harm, so these meetings should take place as soon as possible after suspicions of HBV have been reported. We recommend that at the very least, an HBV child protection strategy meeting should initially be held *within* 14 working days of any initial strategy meeting.

Child Protection Strategy Meeting Attendees

Only those people with significant information to share should attend these meetings. This is extremely pertinent in HBV cases where the potential for information leakage should be minimized. As discussed previously, families are not averse to tasking community members with links to or who are employees of partner agencies to carry out research on the family's behalf linked to the case in question. Law enforcement should always attend these strategy meetings given, in HBV, the potential for serious criminality to have either taken place or to be about to take place. The officer attending should have a good knowledge of the case and an understanding of HBV so that his/her input is meaningful and relevant.

Key Issues to Be Addressed
at All Child Protection Strategy Meetings

There are a number of key issues that need to be addressed at all of the various strategy meetings. These will include the level of risk to the child, in particular, the risk for serious violence to be committed against the child, the risk of removal by family members of the child from the jurisdiction of the strategy meeting members (e.g., the child is taken overseas), or the potential for a child to be moved to another location without the knowledge of the professionals involved in the child's protection. If the child is in care managed by professionals, the strategy meetings will need to explore the risk of family or wider community members locating the child's whereabouts and then conspiring to remove the child from this safe environment or the child herself feeling isolated from her family and or community and returning to the family, thereby placing herself at risk of significant harm.

All parties to strategy meetings should not underestimate the effects of isolation on children who have been removed from their family and the community they know. Children and adults will return to dangerous environments through loneliness, isolation, or failing to recognize/acknowledge the risks to their safety. Where a criminal case is ongoing, then the law enforcement officer attending any strategy meeting should liaise with the officer leading the criminal investigation to ensure that all new material is considered in the context of any future criminal proceedings.

Information Provided to Meetings

Information for a strategy meeting should be provided in a written report summarizing and analyzing the information obtained. We recommend that social services may be the ideal people to provide this report. It is important that those supplying the information distinguish between fact, observation, allegation, and opinion. Where information has come from another source, then this should be made clear in the report without identifying the source.

Child Protection Plan

Where a child or children are at risk, a *child protection plan* needs to be developed and implemented. The purpose of a child protection plan is to arrange and progress the intervention by relevant agencies to improve the well being of the child and reduce the risk of significant harm. A strategy meeting should make recommendations on how agencies, professionals, and possibly family members should work together to safeguard the child's future.

Key Worker

A key worker should be identified, and we recommend that this person comes from social services. He or she, in effect, will become the point of contact for all agencies so that information about the child's welfare is always up to date and shared effectively. It is essential that all new information is contributed to ongoing risk assessment and is assessed in line with the protection plan.

The details and contact of the key worker should be recorded by law enforcement so that it is retrievable quickly and easily. It also is essential for law enforcement to be proactive in obtaining updates from the key worker in respect to information submitted by agency partners. This may include outcomes of home visits, child placement/movement, and child location if taken out of the family home. Initially, we suggest this contact should be weekly given the significant risk associated with HBV; as the enquiry and case matures, this may become monthly. Where there is no new information, a comment should be made by a supervisory law enforcement officer in line with this fact.

Law Enforcement Agencies Responsibilities in Child Protection Meetings

For law enforcement agencies to be effective at any child protection strategy meeting or review, they should undertake some basic actions. We suggest the following represents the minimum standard of preparation for law enforcement officers charged with attending the meeting:

- Ascertain the purpose of the child strategy meeting so that the most suitable officer/unit can attend; as we have stated, given the complexities of HBV, this should be an officer with experience, knowledge, and an understanding of HBV.
- Ascertain if there is a criminal offense involved and if so contact the investigating officer if the investigating officer is not attending.
- Record on the appropriate databases the fact that law enforcement has been invited, who it relates to, and the purpose of the meeting.
- Research all law enforcement indices and databases so that a full picture can be sought of the contact with the child and the family. It should be noted that many children who are victims of HBV are involved in minor criminality, e.g., shop lifting, minor public order, minor violence, or regularly play truant from school or go missing. Therefore, if this is the case, this information also should be considered relevant and brought to strategy meetings.
- Complete a formalized risk assessment of the child and any other children of the family. If the risk is rated as *high*, a risk management plan may need to be put in place prior to attending the meeting; this is especially true if there is an imminent risk of harm to the child. Again, the details of the risk assessment and management plan (if necessary) should be brought to any subsequent meeting.
- Consider restricting any access to law enforcement information on the family and the child. As we have already discussed, families have approached law enforcement staff and officers to search databases to find out information about victims of HBV crimes, especially if those victims no longer live in the family home. This is a real risk and should not be underestimated.
- We recommend that law enforcement should make a point of attending all HBV child strategy meetings because of the very real and significant risks faced by child victims. If law enforcement representatives, for whatever reason, do not attend a meeting, then a full report should be sent to the chair of the strategy/review meeting. The police should also record a robust rationale for nonattendance set against a comprehensive risk assessment

- When a child has a protection plan in place, it is important that law enforcement officers regularly update their relevant databases, with the caveat of placing the necessary restrictions to prevent leakage of information.
- Following child protection strategy meetings, law enforcement should record on relevant databases the reason for the strategy meeting taking place, the outcome of the meeting, details of the risk assessment and risk management plan, the details of professionals and NGOs that may assist in informing future risk assessments and plans, and what administration procedures have been adhered to. At any subsequent meeting, we recommend that the above format is used to record updates.
- When law enforcement agencies attend any meetings, they should have with them all previous known dealings with the family and child.
- If law enforcement agencies have information to share with the meeting that may prejudice a criminal investigation, they should liaise with the chair prior to the meeting to ensure that the information it shares remains confidential. Information of this type should not be shared with the family under any circumstances. If law enforcement is in any doubt about sharing information, advice should be taken from their senior managers and prosecuting lawyers.

Involvement of Family Members in Child Protection Strategy Meetings

For many forms of child abuse, families may often be part of a child protection strategy meeting. However, with HBV cases, we suggest that this should not automatically be the case. This is because of the likely complicity of family members in HBV and the fact that the information shared by professionals could possibly put the child or other individuals in even greater danger from the family. We recommend that if family members are involved in child protection plans, a great deal of caution should be exercised, and a decision to use a family member should be done only after an extensive risk assessment is completed by someone who is experienced and competent in the management of HBV enquiries. It is imperative that professionals have full confidence in the family member to act to protect the child, but it should always be remembered this may then put that family member in danger as well. The decision to exclude families from strategy meetings should rest with the meeting chair, and the family's views, if they so wish, should be communicated to the professionals in attendance by some other means.

Risk Assessment and Management

A child protection strategy meeting should consider if a child is at risk of significant harm and determine an appropriate response in the light of the assessed risk. Risk assessment may follow the protocols described in the risk assessment chapter (7). It is recommended that the child protection strategy is formulated as a written plan that is accepted by all participants to the strategy meeting. This plan should guide the management of the risk a child faces and should include the interventions that will be made.

We would suggest that, where HBV is an issue, there is an increased likelihood of harm, not only for this child, but potentially for other children within the immediate and extended family. Then, drastic interventions, such as removal of the child from the family, should be actively considered and should not necessarily be viewed as a last resort when all else fails.

Child Protection Interventions

Interventions in HBV cases can be quite drastic and, as we have noted above, may involve removing the child from the family home, the community, and geographical area she resides in with her family. While this may seem extreme, in cases where there is a significant risk to the child's well being, it is essential that the child is made as safe as possible and this is likely to be so only when the child is moved away from any possible family or community influence.

When children are removed from the home, this can cause social services and other agencies significant problems because the removal from the home can place the child and those left behind in the family in great danger. Again, such an intervention has to be properly risk assessed and managed to prevent further criminality.

Another important issue is *where* the child/children removed from a family are placed. As we have discussed earlier in this book, there may be other community members sympathetic to HBV living in a locality who may alert the family to the presence of the child/children. The child or children have to be placed where they are no longer in danger. Quite often in HBV cases this will mean moving children away from their family, community, and culture. To ensure that this remains workable in the long term, this needs significant planning and forethought with ongoing regular support. It is noteworthy that depending upon the level of abuse and/or risk the child or children have faced, they may never return to the family home or community.

Whatever intervention is decided on, a significant amount of investment in support will be needed to ensure a child's safety. The chair of the strategy meeting should ensure that all professionals attending understand the recommendations made in the meeting, the requirements of their agencies to fulfill their part of the recommendations, and the level of risk faced by the child. The chair, prior to the conclusion of the meeting, also should set a date for a strategy review meeting.

Child Protection Strategy Review Meeting

It is good practice to hold a child protection strategy review meeting within one month of the first child protection strategy meeting. This is to ensure that momentum is maintained and significant risks are effectively managed. Law enforcement agencies should be represented at all meetings given the risks that HBV presents.

The purpose of the child protection strategy review is to:

- Review the safety of the child set against their protection plan
- Ensure the child remains safe
- Consider whether the current protection plan is adequate or whether amendments are needed given updates in information

The meeting is an opportunity to review all information and updates in respect to the child. This can be a significant and crucial stage in any HBV investigation as the risks to the child can change quite quickly and dramatically, whether the child is living in the family home or is in care. It is critical that prior to any review meeting all participants are up to date with all events, and law enforcement, in particular, has undertaken full research on the child and family on its various indices and databases.

Removal of Child Protection

A major consideration is if and when to remove child protection strategies. Changes to child protection strategies should be made only following a strategy review meeting that involves all stakeholders, and a full written rationale should be produced to justify the decision. In general, we recommend that, in the case of HBV, child protection strategies should be maintained for as long as there is perceived to be a risk to the well being of the child. It is recommended that child protection strategies be removed only when one or more of the factors below pertains:

- The child is no longer at risk of serious harm through the implementation of an effective child protection plan, or a change in family circumstances resulting in removal of the risk.
- The child or the child and family have moved outside the jurisdiction of the review meeting, such as to another area or overseas. Steps should be taken to liaise with relevant agencies in the new area or country the

family has moved to, sharing information with these agencies, and making them aware of the known risks and protection measures.

- The child has reached adulthood or has died, though, in the case of the former, this does not mean the person is no longer at risk of serious harm. Therefore, there may need to be some form of further risk management strategy developed to protect the individual.

Law Enforcement and the Investigation of Child HBV Crimes

Despite the best efforts of child protection, there are occasions when HBV crimes against children do occur. As well as its engagement with multiple agencies in protecting children, where an HBV-related crime has taken place, law enforcement has the additional responsibility of investigating it. In this section, we explore investigative issues that are specific to child HBV crimes. This section should be read in conjunction with the chapters on primary and secondary investigation of HBV (Chapters 3–6).

Investigator Expertise

Given the complexity of HBV, any law enforcement investigation of HBV is likely to be prolonged, thus, managers and supervisors must recognize this and assign investigating officers who have the skills, capability, and capacity to investigate these crimes. We particularly recommend that investigations are conducted by specialist investigators who have expertise in crimes involving children as victims. Such investigators will likely know the relevant legislation associated with children for their jurisdiction, understand the protocols in place between partner agencies to manage the long-term well being of the child, and when undertaking interviews, they will have the relevant skills to achieve the best possible evidence from the child.

Roles of Primary and Secondary Investigation Officers

The roles of primary and secondary investigating officers are similar to those when investigating adult HBV, although there are a number of additional issues that must be considered in cases of child HBV. These are discussed below.

Primary Investigating Officers in Child HBV Offenses

Following a report of HBV, primary investigating officers should check on the welfare of the children, addressing any first aid or medical needs, ascertain the history and intelligence on the family, gather evidence in relation to any offenses against the children, take positive action in securing the safety of the children, identify any immediate risks to the child, and manage the risks effectively before handing the matter over to a secondary investigator. Primary investigating officers should not leave the children in a situation where their safety cannot be assured and they should not use the child as an interpreter where language is an issue.

Secondary Investigating Officers in Child HBV Offenses

Secondary investigating officers should identify any gaps in the evidential and intelligence chains so that all pertinent information can be shared with relevant partners. This will allow for a fuller and more detailed picture to develop so that intervention and risk management measures are appropriate to the case in hand. This is not withstanding the duty of a secondary investigator to secure evidence.

Use of Intelligence

It is important that all law enforcement officers, regardless of their special-ism, record and disseminate *any* intelligence they have relating to an HBV allegation regardless of how they come about the information. All intelligence should be reviewed and evaluated; where gaps are identified, work should be undertaken to address the gaps. It also is essential where other information becomes known during an investigation outside of their sphere of work but impacting on other police areas, such as terrorism, organized crime, sexual offending, etc., then the investigating officers must record and disseminate this information. The authors are aware of some HBV perpetrators who also have been involved in other unrelated criminality. HBV criminality should not be seen in isolation and where other unrelated offenses are identified, then the police should deal with them as directed by their local working protocols.

Geographical Transience

As we have discussed, HBV crimes can be geographically transient in that victims, especially children, can be moved to different areas to facilitate HBV offenses. As a result, the law enforcement investigating units for HBV allega-tions may not be geographically located where the child lives. In these cases, a decision needs to be made in line with local protocols as to who is best placed to investigate, in particular, whether this will be a joint investigation between the local law enforcement and those based where the child lives, and what partnership intervention should look like. We would recommend that where possible the most appropriate investigation unit would be the one that is best able to meet the child's best interests. This, of course, may vary depending on many factors, such as knowledge of the child and/or their fam-ily, expertise, and availability of staff.

Conclusion

As we have discussed, dealing with child victims of HBV presents a number of specific challenges and requires agencies to work together, sharing information, and developing workable strategies that aim to protect children above all else. All agencies need to recognize the risks children face, the complexities of HBV, and what processes and partnership support is available. Hopefully, we have built upon the reader's knowledge of HBV by showing how it affects children and have introduced some concepts that will assist agencies in managing these significant risks.

Concluding Remarks   11

In this book, we have attempted to give an overview of the current state of knowledge about honor-based violence (HBV) and how this can be applied to policing and prevention. As we have noted, HBV is a complex issue requiring carefully considered strategies to combat it. In this final chapter, we wish to provide a brief summary of what we have discussed in order to illustrate both what we know and what we don't yet know about HBV, and provide some suggestions for future work and some key take-home messages.

Defining HBV

In the first chapter, we attempted to define HBV. As we noted, the academic and professional literatures are currently far from agreement about how best to define HBV. This state of affairs is a problem, especially for practitioners and for policy makers trying to understand and make use of the literature. Different definitions make it difficult to compare research findings or the efficacy of interventions that are based on a particular definition. Even worse, varied definitions may lead to a failure to identify HBV with a risk that victims may be harmed.

In this book, we used the ACPO (Association of Chief Police Officers) definition of HBV: "*A crime or incident, which has or may have been committed to protect or defend the honor of the family and/or community*" (ACPO, 2010a), so that we would be as inclusive as possible.

However, whilst this definition may be useful for a practical guide such as this, it may be too broad. For example, by this definition, potentially a wide range of illegal acts are included as HBV; essentially any action motivated by honor concerns could be HBV. This means, for example, that Mafia executions and certain forms of gang violence could be included. While such illegal acts may be motivated by honor, it is not traditionally the sort of family-oriented violence that most practitioners would recognize as HBV. We have explicitly ignored gang and similar violence in this book. Another issue is that too narrow a definition of HBV is also a problem because this may mean that certain types of illegal acts, victims, or offenders are excluded from consideration. For example, some definitions regard HBV as a form of male violence against women explicitly excluding male victims and female perpetrators from consideration.

We argue that, in order to improve our ability to identify and prevent HBV, there should be an attempt to achieve consensus on a definition. In our view, this definition needs to be broad enough to encompass the range of illegal acts described in this book, but narrow enough to avoid capturing otherwise unrelated behavior. As a start, we recommend that the familial nature of HBV should be made explicit in any definition to differentiate it from other forms of violence. Also, the definition should be gender neutral to avoid ignoring certain types of victims or offenders.

Explaining HBV

In Chapter 2 we discussed, at some length, explanatory theories of HBV. As we noted, theorizing and etiological research into HBV is in its infancy, and so the model we suggested should be regarded as speculative. It is important to stress again that for a theory of HBV to have real value it must take into account multiple levels of explanation, from cultural forces that shape beliefs and attitudes concerning the legitimacy and desirability of certain behavior, through the meanings that cultural messages have for individuals, to how individuals perceive their situation and the resulting emotions they experience. As we discussed, single-factor theories that propose that HBV is caused by one factor, such as culture or gender, are too simplistic and don't account for what research evidence there is. Indeed, it is too simplistic and runs the risk of stigmatizing communities, simply to argue that HBV occurs only in certain cultures. Similarly, to argue that HBV is simply an example of male violence against women misses the nuanced nature of this offending.

The model we suggested in Chapter 2 accounts for many observations concerning HBV and is based upon existing social psychological models, such as the *theory of planned behavior,* that are concerned with human social behavior in general. However, the model is a descriptive model and requires empirical testing to validate its assumptions. The model, however, does provide hypotheses that can be tested by collecting relevant data. So, for example, future research could explore the attitudes and beliefs of perpetrators of HBV and compare them to those of individuals from similar cultures who do not engage in HBV with the expectation, drawn from the model, that perpetrators should have more beliefs and attitudes supportive of HBV than non-perpetrators. In a similar vein, future work should attempt to explore why it is that some individuals do not commit HBV despite having similar cultural experiences. Identifying reasons for this may contribute to the development of HBV prevention.

Investigation, Risk Assessment, and Management of HBV

In Chapters 3 through 10, we explored the investigation of HBV allegations and the assessment and management of risk. Many of the suggestions made are those that underlie best investigative practice for law enforcement and multiagency working, in general. However, there are some important caveats of illegal acts that are motivated by familial honor for which investigators and agencies need to be aware.

Risk of Harm

There is a high risk of harm for individuals living in families that are supportive of HBV. This risk is heightened following a report to authorities of HBV victimization. This means that even where no offense has been committed but where individuals report their fear that HBV may happen to them, investigators should take this very seriously and take steps to protect these individuals. Indeed, research consistently shows that victim fear is a very good predictor of violence.

Give this proper risk, assessment is vital to the successful investigation and management of HBV allegations. There are some risk assessment tools for HBV, notably the DASH tool; however, more research is needed to further improve such tools and identify reliable predictors of violence. In addition, when an individual reports his/her fears or experience of HBV and where there are several children in a family, investigators need to recognize that the other children also may be at risk of HBV and need to act accordingly to protect them.

Risk Management

Management of risk is vital for all agencies involved in HBV and we have discussed some useful strategies in this regard. However, what we describe is not the last word in managing HBV and we recommend that agencies regularly review the risk management methods they use in light of emerging research to better protect victims.

The cultural context of HBV raises many issues for agencies dealing with it. Many of the tried and tested methods of managing child abuse or family violence actually place victims at increased risk, e.g., involving family members in decisions about child protection or moving victims to an area that is of a similar cultural mix to the one they came from. Agencies need to recognize that HBV is not like other forms of family violence and some solutions will necessarily entail new approaches, such as not informing families of a victim's whereabouts.

Cultural Sensitivity and Managing HBV

One issue that many individuals struggle with is the tendency to judge an event or situation through the lens of their own experience and values. This is something that is not advisable when considering HBV. To do so risks disbelieving that parents could injure or kill their child simply for wearing makeup or having a boyfriend that is unacceptable. This, in turn, may predicate disbelief of a victim's claims or a tendency to accept a perpetrator's explanations. Likewise, a fear of upsetting cultural traditions or of being accused of racism also has stopped agencies from acting against HBV. As we noted, none of the acts that we have classed as HBV are sanctioned by any religion and the vast majority of people regard them with revulsion, regardless from what culture they originate. While it is important not to demonize communities or cultures or attack their traditions just because they differ from one's own, agencies should focus upon the suffering of victims and be bold in their attempts to protect them.

Communication

In Chapter 9, we stressed the importance of communication in our attempts to prevent HBV. Communication impacts professionals in terms of giving them the skills to identify HBV victimization and communities in signaling that HBV is unacceptable. It also impacts individual members of agencies in detailing with the agency's response to HBV. We noted that, for messages to have maximal impact upon the receiver, they need to be consistent and unambiguous. The characteristics of the communicator are important as well in maximizing the impact of the message as the communicator should be regarded as acceptable to the audience. Agencies, therefore, need to be sensitive to the messages that they communicate and the method of communication and the communicator.

Children and HBV

In Chapter 10, we discussed the experience of children and HBV. We noted that children are frequently at high risk of all forms of HBV, largely because they are dependent upon family members for their well being. We highlighted some best practice approaches for agencies in dealing with child HBV cases and stressed that prevention of harm should be the primary motive of all agencies. In order to achieve this, different agencies need to develop clear policies and protocols governing how they work together in a spirit of mutual cooperation.

Concluding Comments

Honor-based violence is many faceted and provides law enforcement and other agencies with many challenges. We think agencies should be under no illusions about the risk of extreme violence faced by victims of HBV and should do everything in their power to protect them. We think that despite these risks HBV can be prevented, but to do this successfully requires agencies to be sensitive to its characteristics, sensitive to the ways they engage with victims, witnesses, perpetrators, and communities, and systematic in their approaches to investigation and management.

Finally, we hope that this book has enhanced the reader's knowledge and understanding of HBV and will help in developing appropriate interventions. As we said at the beginning of the book, if it helps to reduce the suffering caused by HBV or even saves just one life, then we will have achieved everything we hoped for in writing it.

References

Abu-Lughod, L, (2011). Seductions of honor crime. *Differences: A journal of feminist cultural studies, 22*(1), 17–63.

Ajzen, I. (1992). Persuasive communication theory in social psychology: A historic perspective. In M. J. Manfredo (Ed.), *Influencing human behaviour: Theory and applications*. Champaign, IL: Sagemore Publishing.

Ajzen, I. (2011). The theory of planned behaviour: Reactions and reflections. *Psychology & Health, 26*(9), 1113–1127.

Anderson, E. (1994). The code of the streets. *The Atlantic Monthly, 5*, 81–94.

Arata, C. M., Langhinrichsen-Rohling, J., Bowers, D., & O'Farrill-Swails, L. (2005). Single versus multi-type maltreatment: An examination of the long-term effects of child abuse. *Journal of Aggression, Maltreatment & Trauma, 11*(4), 29–52.

Association of Chief Police Officers (ACPO). (2005). *Core investigative doctrine*. London: National Policing Improvement Agency (NPIA).

Association of Chief Police Officers (ACPO). (2009). *DASH*. London: (NPIA).

Association of Chief Police Officers (ACPO). (2010a). *Honor-based violence strategy*. London: National Policing Improvement Agency (NPIA).

Association of Chief Police Officers (ACPO). (2010b). *Murder manual*. London: National Policing Improvement Agency (NPIA).

Association of Chief Police Officers (ACPO). (2012). *Family liaison officer guidance*. London: National Policing Improvement Agency (NPIA).

Breakwell, G. (Ed.). (1982). *Threatened identities*. London: John Wiley & Sons.

Burke, P. J. (1991). Identity processes and social stress. *American Sociological Review, 56*, 836–849.

Burke, P. J. (2003). *Advances in identity theory and research*. New York: Springer Publishing.

Centre for Social Cohesion. (2010). *Crimes of the community. Honour based violence in the UK*. London: Centre for Social Cohesion.

Chesler, P. (2010). Worldwide trends in honor killings. *Middle East Quarterly*, Spring, 3–11

Cohen, D. (1998). Culture, social organization, and patterns of violence. *Journal of Personality and Social Psychology, 75*(2), 408.

Cohen, D., Vandello, J. A., & Rantilla, A. K. (1998). The sacred and the social: Cultures of honor and violence. In P. Gilbert & B. Andrews (Eds.), *Shame: Interpersonal behavior, psychopathology, and culture*. New York: Oxford University Press.

Cohen, D., Vandello, J. A., Puente, S., & Rantilla, A. K. (1999). "When you call me that, smile!" How norms for politeness, interaction styles, and aggression work together in southern culture. *Social Psychology Quarterly, 62*, 257–275.

Coomaraswamy, R, (2005). Honor crimes. In S. Hossain & L. Welchman, L. (Eds.). *'Honour': Crimes, paradigms and violence against women*. London: Zed Books.

Crown Prosecution Service. (2008). *Forced marriage and HBV crimes*. London: CPS.

Department for Children, Schools, and Families. (2009). *Forced marriage—Prevalence and service response*. Research Report No. DCSF-RR128. London: DCSF.

Fischer, D. M. (1989). Albion's seed. New York: OU Press.

Fossum, M. A., & Mason, M. J. (1986). *Facing shame: Families in recovery*. New York: WW Norton & Company.

Gilbert, P. & Andrews, B. (Eds.).(1998). *Shame: Interpersonal behavior, psychopathology and culture*. New York: Oxford University Press.

Gill, A. (2004). Voicing the silent fear: South Asian women's experiences of domestic violence. *The Howard Journal of Criminal Justice, 43*(5), 465–483.

Gill, A., & Anthia, S. (2011). *Forced marriage: Introducing a social justice and human rights perspective*. London: Zed Books.

Gilmore, D. D. (1991). *Manhood in the making: Cultural concepts of masculinity*. New Haven, CT: Yale University Press.

Johnson, L. L., & Lipsett-Rivera, S. (1998). *The faces of honor: Sex, shame, and violence*. Albuquerque: University of New Mexico Press.

Her Majesty's Government. (2007). *Forced marriage civil protection act* 2007. London, United Kingdom.

Hossain, S., & Welchman, L. (Eds.). (2005). *'Honour': Crimes, paradigms and violence against women*. London: Zed Books.

Human Rights Watch. (2001). *Violence against women and "honor" crimes*. Online at: http://www.hrw.org/press/2001/04/un_oral12_0405.htm (accessed May 12, 2012).

Johal, A. (2003). Struggle not submission: Domestic violence in the 1990s. In R. Gupta (Ed.), *From homebreakers to jailbreakers*. London: Zed Books.

Karma Nirvana. (2004). *Honor violence*. Paper presented at Kirklees Council Conference on Honor Killing, Huddersfield, April.

Marshall, H., & Yazdani, A. (1999). Locating culture in accounting for self-harm amongst Asian young women. *Journal of Community & Applied Social Psychology, 9*(6), 413–433.

McKenzie, K., Bhui, K., Nanchalal, K. & Blizard, B. (2008). Suicide rates in people of South Asian origin in England and Wales: 1993-2003. *The British Journal of Psychiatry, 193*: 406–409.

Meetoo, V., & Mirza, H. S. (2007). There is nothing honorable about honor killings: Gender and violence and the limits of multiculturalism. *Women's Studies International Forum, 30*, 187–200.

Mischel, W. (1992). *Personality and assessment*. New York: John Wiley & Sons.

Nisbett, R. E., & Cohen, D. (1996). *Culture of honor: The psychology of violence in the South*. Boulder, CO: Westview Press.

Pitt-Rivers, J. (1966). *Honour and social status*. In J. G. Peristany (Ed.). *Honor and shame* (pp. 19–77). Chicago: University of Chicago Press.

Roberts, K. A. (2011). *A multi-level model for protecting victims and investigating perpetrators*. Paper presented at Honor Killings Across Culture and Time Conference, Canberra, Australia.

Roberts, K. A., & Herrington, V. (2011). Police interviews with suspects. In J. Kitaeff (ed.). *Handbook of police psychology*. Boca Raton, FL: Taylor & Francis.

Schneider, J. (1971). Of vigilance and virgins: Honor, shame and access to resources in Mediterranean societies. *Ethnology*, 1–24.

Shepherd, E. (1993). Ethical interviewing. *Issues in Criminological & Legal Psychology, 18*, 46–56.

Smartt, U. 2006. Honour killings. *Justice of the Peace Journal, 170*, 4–7.

Stets, J. E., & Burke, P. J. (2000). Identity theory and social identity theory. *Social Psychology Quarterly*, 224–237.

Stryker, S., & Burke, P. J. (2000). The past, present, and future of an identity theory. *Social Psychology Quarterly*, 284–297.

Tangney, J. P., Miller, R. S., Flicker, L., & Barlow, D. H. (1996). Are shame, guilt, and embarrassment distinct emotions? *Journal of Personal Social Psychology, 70*(6), 1256–1269,

Triandis, H. C. (1994). *Culture and social behavior*. New York: McGraw-Hill.

Tyler, T. R. (2006). Legitimacy and legitimization. *Annual Review of Psychology, 57*, 375–400.

UNICEF. (2010). *Global databases based on data from Multiple Indicator Cluster Survey, Demographic and Health Survey, and other national surveys, 1997–2009.* New York.

United Kingdom Home Office. (1984). *Police and criminal evidence act*. London.

United Kingdom Home Office. (2000). *A choice by right: The report of the working group on forced marriage*. London.

United Kingdom Home Office. (2002). OASys User Manual, Volume 2. London: HO Communication Directorate.

United Kingdom Foreign and Commonwealth Office. (2009). *Multi-agency practice guidelines: Handling cases of forced marriage*, London: FCO.

United Kingdom Foreign and Commonwealth Office. (2011). *Multiagency practice guidelines: Female genital mutilation*. London: FCO.

United Nations. (1948). *Article 16(1) & (2) of the Universal Declaration of Human Rights*. New York: United Nations.

United Nations. (1970). *General Recommendation 21, Comment Article 16(1)(b) United Nations convention on the elimination of all forms of discrimination against women*. New York: United Nations.

United Nations. (1989). *Article 34 United Nations convention on the rights of the child*. New York: United Nations.

United Nations. (2000). *Ending violence against women and girls*. State of the World Population. New York: United Nations.

Vandello, J. A., & Cohen, D. (2003). Male honor and female fidelity: Implicit cultural scripts that perpetuate domestic violence. *Journal of Personality and Social Psychology, 84*(5), 997.

Vandello, J. A., & Cohen, D. (2004). When believing is seeing: Sustaining norms of violence in cultures of honor. *The psychological foundations of culture*, 281.

Walby, S. (1990). *Theorizing patriarchy*. Oxford, U.K.: Blackwell.

World Health Organization. (2012). *Female genital mutilation key facts*. Online at: http://www.who.int/mediacentre/factsheets/fs241/en/ (accessed May 7, 2012).

Index

A

Abortion, sex-selective, 3
Accepting risk, 123
Access to crime scenes, 49
Acid attacks, 11–12
ACPO (U.K.)
    DASH tool, 120–122
    definition of honor-based violence, 2
Actual behavioral control, 35
    honor-based cultures, 36–37
Ad hoc supervision, review and, 106
Adult social services, multiagency
    cooperation and, 136–137
Age
    definition of a child, 149
    HBV crime type and, 149
    victims, 69
Agencies, involvement of with children
    HBV victims, 157
Arranged marriage, distinction of from
    forced marriage, 7
Arrest of suspects, 54–55, 103
    decision concerning, 79–80
    staff requirements for, 81
    strategies for, 80–81
Arresting officers
    briefing of, 81
    debriefing of, 82
Assault, patterns of, 90
Attitude, 35
    effect of honor-related cultural norms
        on, 36
    law enforcement and HBV victims,
        41–42
Attractiveness of communicator, 147
Avoiding risk, 122–123
Awareness, risk aversion and, 125

B

Barriers to reporting HBV, 139–140
Behavioral beliefs, 34–35

effect of honor-related cultural norms
    on, 36
Behaviors
    development of cultural norms and,
        23–24
    law enforcement and HBV victims,
        41–42
Blood distribution, 64
Blood feuds, 12
Bride price, 6–7
Briefing
    arresting officers, 81
    interviewers, 83
Building block principles of investigation,
    39–40

C

Charging suspects, 84–85
Child abduction, 153
Child abuse and neglect, female children, 4
Child neglect, 155–156
Child protection interventions, 166–167
    removal of, 167–168
Child protection strategy meetings
    information provided to, 163
    involvement of family members in, 165
    key issues addressed at, 162–163
    purpose of, 161
    responsibilities of law enforcement
        agencies in, 164–165
    review meetings, 167
    risk assessment and management, 166
    timing of, 162
Child victimization investigations, key
        workers for, 163
Children
    as witnesses, 111
    definition of, 149
    domestic violence and, 154–155 (*See also*
        Domestic violence)
    emotional abuse of, 155

International Police Executive Symposium (IPES)

The *International Police Executive Symposium* (IPES)* was founded in 1994. The aims and objectives of the IPES are to provide a forum to foster closer relationships among police researchers and practitioners globally, to facilitate cross cultural, international and interdisciplinary exchanges for the enrichment of the law enforcement profession, and to encourage discussion and published research on challenging and contemporary topics related to the profession.

One of the most important activities of the IPES is the organization of an annual meeting under the auspices of a police agency or an educational institution. Every year, since 1994, annual meetings have been hosted by such agencies and institutions all over the world. Past hosts have included the Canton Police of Geneva, Switzerland; the International Institute of the Sociology of Law, Onati, Spain; Kanagawa University, Yokohama, Japan; the Federal Police, Vienna, Austria; the Dutch Police and Europol, The Hague, The Netherlands; the Andhra Pradesh Police, India; the Center for Public Safety, Northwestern University, United States; the Polish Police Academy, Szczytno, Poland; the Police of Turkey (twice); the Kingdom of Bahrain Police; a group of institutions in Canada (consisting of the University of the Fraser Valley, Abbotsford Police Department, Royal Canadian Mounted Police, the Vancouver Police Department, the Justice Institute of British Columbia, Canadian Police College, and the International Centre for Criminal Law Reform and Criminal Justice Policy); the Czech Police Academy, Prague; the Dubai Police; the Ohio

* www.ipes.info

Association of Chiefs of Police and the Cincinnati Police Department, Ohio, United States; the Republic of Macedonia and the Police of Malta.

The 2011 Annual Meeting on the theme of "Policing Violence, Crime, Disorder and Discontent: International Perspectives" was hosted in Buenos Aires, Argentina, on June 26–30, 2011. The 2012 annual meeting was hosted at United Nations in New York on the theme of "Economic Development, Armed Violence and Public Safety" on August 5–10. The 2013 Annual Meeting on the theme of "Global Issues in Contemporary Policing" will be hosted by the Ministry of Interior of Hungary and the Hungarian National Police on August 4–9, 2013.

There also have been occasional special meetings of IPES. A special meeting was co-hosted by the Bavarian Police Academy of Continuing Education in Ainring, Germany, University of Passau, Germany, and State University of New York, Plattsburgh, in 2000. The second special meeting was hosted by the police in the Indian state of Kerala. The third special meeting on the theme of "Contemporary Issues in Public Safety and Security" was hosted by the commissioner of police of the Blekinge Region of Sweden and the president of the University of Technology on August 10–14, 2011.

The majority of participants of the annual meetings are usually directly involved in the police profession. In addition, scholars and researchers in the field also participate. The meetings comprise both structured and informal sessions to maximize dialogue and exchange of views and information. The executive summary of each meeting is distributed to participants as well as to a wide range of other interested police professionals and scholars. In addition, a book of selected papers from each annual meeting is published through CRC Press/Taylor & Francis Group, Prentice Hall, Lexington Books, and other reputed publishers. A special issue of *Police Practice and Research: An International Journal* also is published with the most thematically relevant papers after the usual blind review process.

IPES Institutional Supporters

Australian Institute of Police Management, Collins Beach Road Manly NSW 2095, Australia, (contact Connie Coniglio). +612 9934 4800; Fax: +612 9934 4780; email: cconiglio@aipm.gov.au

APCOF, The African Policing Civilian Oversight Forum, (contact Sean Tait), 2nd floor, The Armoury, Buchanan Square, 160 Sir Lowry Road, Woodstock Cape Town, 8000 South Africa. 27 21 461 7211; Fax: 27 21 461 7213; email: sean@apcof.org.za

Baker College of Jackson, 2800 Springport Road, Jackson, MI 49202, U.S. (contact: Blaine Goodrich) 517-841-4522; email: blaine. goodrich@baker.edu

Cyber Defense & Research Initiatives (contact James Lewis), LLC, PO Box 86, Leslie, MI 49251, U.S. 517-242-6730; email: lewisja@cyberdefenseresearch.com

Defendology Center for Security, Sociology and Criminology Research (Valibor Lalic), Srpska Street 63,78000 Banja Luka, Bosnia and Herzegovina. 38751-308-914 (phone and fax); email: lalicv@teol.net

Department of Criminal Justice (Dr. Harvey L. McMurray, Chair), North Carolina Central University, 301 Whiting Criminal Justice Bldg., Durham, NC 27707, U.S. 919-530-5204, 919-530-7909; Fax: 919-530-5195; email: hmcmurray@nccu.edu.

Cliff Roberson, Professor Emeritus, Washburn University, 16307 Sedona Woods, Houston, TX 77082-1665, U.S. 713-703-6639; Fax: 281-596-8483; email: roberson37@msn.com

De Montfort University, Health and Life Sciences, School of Applied Social Sciences (Dr. Perry Stanislas, Hirsh Sethi), Hawthorn Building, The Gateway, Leicester, LE1 9BH, U.K. 44 (0) 116 257 7146; email: pstanislas@dmu.ac.uk, hsethi@dmu.ac.uk

Department of Psychology (Stephen Perrott), Mount Saint Vincent University, 166 Bedford Highway, Halifax, Nova Scotia, Canada. email: Stephen.perrott@mvsu.ca

Fayetteville State University (Dr. David E. Barlow, Professor and Dean), College of Basic and Applied Sciences, 130 Chick Building, 1200 Murchison Road, Fayetteville, NC, 28301 U.S. 910-672-1659; Fax: 910-672-1083; email: dbarlow@uncfsu.edu

Edmundo Oliveira, PhD, 1 Irving Place University Tower Apt. U 7 A 10003.9723, New York, New York. 407-342-24.73; email: edmundooliveira@cfl.rr.com.

International Council on Security and Development (ICOS) (Andre Souza, Senior Researcher), Visconde de Piraja 577/605, Ipanema, Rio de Janeiro 22410–003, Brazil. 55 21 3186 5444; email: asouza@icosgroup.net

Justice Studies Department, San Jose State University, 1 Washington Square, San Jose, CA 95192-0050; (Mark E. Correia, PhD, Chair and Associate Professor), mcorreia@casa.sjsu.edu. 408-924-1350; Kerala Police (Shri Balasubramaniyum, Director General of Police), Police Headquarters, Trivandrum, Kerala, India. email: manojabraham05@gmail.com

Law School, John Moores University (David Lowe, LLB Program Leader), Law School, Redmonds Building, Brownlow Hill, Liverpool, L3 5UG, U.K. 44 (0) 151 231 3918; email: D.Lowe@ljmu.ac.uk

Molloy College, The Department of Criminal Justice (contact Dr. John A. Eterno, NYPD Captain Ret.), 1000 Hempstead Avenue, PO Box 5002, Rockville Center, NY 11571-5002, U.S. 516-678-5000, ext. 6135; Fax: 516-256-2289; email: jeterno@molloy.edu

National Institute of Criminology and Forensic Science (Kamalendra Prasad, Inspector General of Police), MHA, Outer Ring Road, Sector 3, Rohini, Delhi 110085, India. 91 11 275 2 5095; Fax: 91 11 275 1 0586; email: director.nicfs@nic.in

National Police Academy, Japan (Naoya Oyaizu, Deputy Director), Police Policy Research Center, 183-8558: 3-12-1 Asahi-cho Fuchu-city, Tokyo, Japan. 8142 354 3550; Fax: 8142 330 3550; email: PPRC@npa.go.jp

Royal Canadian Mounted Police (Craig J. Callens), 657 West 37th Ave., Vancouver, BC V5Z 1K6, Canada. 604-264-2003; Fax: 604-264-3547; email: bcrcmp@rcmp-grc.gc.ca

School of Psychology and Social Science, Head, Social Justice Research Centre (Prof. S. Caroline Taylor, Foundation Chair in Social Justice), Edith Cowan University, 270 Joondalup Drive, Joondalup, WA 6027, Australia. email: c.taylor@ecu.edu.au

South Australia Police (Commissioner Mal Hyde), Office of the Commissioner, South Australia Police, 30 Flinders Street, Adelaide, SA 5000, Australia. email: mal.hyde@police.sa.gov.au

Southeast Missouri State University (Dr. Diana Bruns, Dean), Criminal Justice & Sociology, One University Plaza, Cape Girardeau, MO 63701, U.S. 573-651-2178; email: dbruns@semo.edu

The Faculty of Criminal Justice and Security (Dr. Gorazd Meško), University of Maribor, Kotnikova 8,1000 Ljubljana, Slovenia. 3861 300 83 39; Fax: 3861 2302 687; email: gorazd.mesko@fvv.uni-mb.si

UNISA, Department of Police Practice (Setlhomamaru Dintwe), Florida Campus; Cnr Christiaan DeWet and Pioneer Avenues, Private Bag X6, 1710 South Africa. 011 471 2116; Cell: 083 581 6102; Fax: 011 471 2255; email: Dintwsi@unisa.ac.za

University of Maine at Augusta, College of Natural and Social Sciences (Richard Myers, Prof.), 46 University Drive, Augusta, ME 04330-9410, U.S. email: rmyers@maine.edu

University of New Haven (Dr. Mario Gaboury, School of Criminal Justice and Forensic Science), 300 Boston Post Road, West Haven, CT 06516, U.S. 203-932-7260; email: rward@newhaven.edu

University of South Africa, College of Law (Professor Kris Pillay, School of Criminal Justice, Director), Preller Street, Muckleneuk, Pretoria. email: cpillay@unisa.ac.za

University of the Fraser Valley (Dr. Darryl Plecas), Department of Criminology & Criminal Justice, 33844 King Road, Abbotsford, British Columbia V2S7M9, Canada. 604-853-7441; Fax: 604-853-9990; email: Darryl. plecas@ufv.ca

University of West Georgia (David A. Jenks, PhD), Pafford Building 2309, 1601 Maple Street, Carrollton, GA 30118, U.S. 678-839-6327; email: djenks@westga.edu

A Call for Authors
Advances in Police Theory and Practice

AIMS AND SCOPE:

This cutting-edge series is designed to promote publication of books on contemporary advances in police theory and practice. We are especially interested in volumes that focus on the nexus between research and practice, with the end goal of disseminating innovations in policing. We will consider collections of expert contributions as well as individually authored works. Books in this series will be marketed internationally to both academic and professional audiences. This series also seeks to —

Police Reform
in China

Mission-Based
Policing

The International
Trafficking of Human
Organs

- Bridge the gap in knowledge about advances in theory and practice regarding who the police are, what they do, and how they maintain order, administer laws, and serve their communities
- Improve cooperation between those who are active in the field and those who are involved in academic research so as to facilitate the application of innovative advances in theory and practice

The series especially encourages the contribution of works coauthored by police practitioners and researchers. We are also interested in works comparing policing approaches and methods globally, examining such areas as the policing of transitional states, democratic policing, policing and minorities, preventive policing, investigation, patrolling and response, terrorism, organized crime and drug enforcement. In fact, every aspect of policing, public safety, and security, as well as public order is relevant for the series. Manuscripts should be between 300 and 600 printed pages. If you have a proposal for an original work or for a contributed volume, please be in touch.

Series Editor
Dilip Das, Ph.D., Ph: 802-598-3680
E-mail: dilipkd@aol.com

Dr. Das is a professor of criminal justice and Human Rights Consultant to the United Nations. He is a former chief of police, and founding president of the International Police Executive Symposium, IPES, www.ipes.info. He is also founding editor-in-chief of *Police Practice and Research: An International Journal* (PPR), (Routledge/Taylor & Francis), www.tandf.co.uk/journals. In addition to editing the *World Police Encyclopedia* (Taylor & Francis, 2006), Dr. Das has published numerous books and articles during his many years of involvement in police practice, research, writing, and education.

Proposals for the series may be submitted to the series editor or directly to –
Carolyn Spence
Senior Editor • CRC Press / Taylor & Francis Group
561-317-9574 • 561-997-7249 (fax)
carolyn.spence@taylorandfrancis.com • www.crcpress.com
6000 Broken Sound Parkway NW, Suite 300, Boca Raton, FL 33487